# From Political Economy to Anthropology

*For Walter C. Neale*

# From Political Economy to Anthropology

*Situating Economic Life in Past Societies*

---

*Volume 3*
*Critical Perspectives on Historic Issues*

---

Edited by Colin A.M. Duncan
and David W. Tandy

Montréal/New York
London

Copyright © 1994 BLACK ROSE BOOKS LTD.

No part of this book may be reproduced or transmitted in any form, by any means — electronic or mechanical, including photocopying and recording, or by any information storage or retrieval system — without written permission from the publisher, or, in the case of photocopying or other reprographic copying, a licence from the Canadian Reprography Collective, with the exception of brief passages quoted by a reviewer in a newspaper or magazine.

BLACK ROSE BOOKS No. X213
Hardcover 1-895431-89-1
Paperback1-895431-88-3

Library of Congress No. 93-73927

Canadian Cataloguing in Publication Data

Main entry under title
Anthropology to political economy: situating economic life in past societies
(Critical perspectives on historic issues; 3)

ISBN 1-895431-89-1 (bound)
ISBN 1-895431-88-3 (pbk.)

1. Economics — Sociological aspects.
2. Economic history. I. Duncan, Colin A.M. (Colin Adrien MacKinley), 1954 – . II. Tandy, David W. III. Series

HC31.A68 1993   306.3   C93-090627-6

Mailing Address

BLACK ROSE BOOKS
C.P. 1258
Succ. Place du Parc
Montréal, Québec
H2W 2R3 Canada

BLACK ROSE BOOKS
340 Nagel Drive
Cheektowaga, New York
14225 USA

Printed in Canada

*A publication of the Institute of Policy Alternatives of Montréal*
(IPAM)

# Contents

| | |
|---|---:|
| Acknowledgments | vi |
| Notes on Contributors | vii |

Introduction
*Colin A.M. Duncan and David W. Tandy* ............ 1

1. Karl Polanyi's Distinctive Approach to Social Analysis and the Case of Ancient Greece: Ideas, Criticisms, Consequences
   *David W. Tandy and Walter C. Neale* ............ 9

2. Chief and Followers In Pre-State Greece
   *Walter Donlan* ............ 34

3. The Community Against the Market in Classical Athens
   *Ian Morris* ............ 52

4. The Institutional Theory of Trade and the Organization of Intersocial Commerce In Ancient Athens
   *John Adams* ............ 80

5. Water Management as a Function of Locational and Appropriational Movements and the Case of the Classic Maya of Tikal
   *Vernon L. Scarborough* ............ 105

6. *Hansatsu*: Local Currencies in Pre-Industrial Japan
   *Makoto Maruyama* ............ 122

7. Potatoes, Muskets, and a Changing Community: How the Changing Economic Roles of Women and Slaves Remained Embedded in Maori Society, 1769-1839
   *William C. Schaniel* ............ 133

8. Exposure and Protection: The Double Movement in the Economic History of Rural India
   *Walter C. Neale* ............ 149

9. Time and the Economy in a Northeastern Kentucky Region
   *Rhoda Halperin* ............ 170

# Acknowledgements

The editors would like to thank a number of people for helping in various ways to get this book completed. For inviting us to put this volume together, we thank Marguerite Mendell of the Karl Polanyi Institute of Political Economy, the General Editor of this series. We thank also her assistant Ana Gomez. For important technical assistance we would like to thank Abraham Rotstein in Toronto, Bill Joslin and J. Bruce MacNaughton in Kingston, and Christina Bucher, Chauncey J. Mellor, and Bobbie Owenby in Knoxville. Alessandra Duncan continued to provide her usual cheerful personal and financial support of Polanyiphilic activities. Both editors wish to acknowledge many years of collaboration, inspiration, and friendship by dedicating this volume to Walter C. Neale.

# Notes on Contributors

**John Adams**, professor and chair of economics at Northeastern University, is the author of many articles on institutional economics, as well as several books, among them (with Wendell C. Gordon) *Economics as Social Science: An Evolutionary Approach* (Riverdale, MD: Riverdale Company, 1989) and (with Sabiha Iqbal) *Exports, Politics, and Economic Development: Pakistan, 1970-1982* (Boulder, CO: Westview Press, 1983).

**Walter Donlan** is professor of classics at the University of California at Irvine. In addition to his many important articles on early Greece and Homer, he is the author of *The Aristocratic Ideal in Ancient Greece* (Lawrence, KA: Coronado Press, 1980). He is currently at work on an extensive study of Dark Age Greece.

**Colin A.M. Duncan** teaches in the Department of History at Queen's University in Kingston, Ontario. He is the author of many articles on the agricultural history of Britain and of *The Centrality of Agriculture: Between Humankind and the Rest of Nature* (Montréal and Kingston: McGill-Queen's University Press, 1994).

**Rhoda Halperin** is professor of anthropology at the University of Cincinnati. Her latest books are *The Livelihood of Kin: Making Ends meet "The Kentucky Way"* (Austin: University of Texas Press, 1990) and *Cultural Economies Past and Present* (Austin: University of Texas Press, 1994).

**Makoto Maruyama** teaches political economy and economic anthropology in the Department of Social Sciences at the University of Tokyo.

**Ian Morris** is associate professor in the Departments of History and Classics at the University of Chicago. His books include *Burial and Ancient Society: The Rise of the Greek City-State* (Cambridge:

Cambridge University Press, 1987) and *Death-Ritual and Social Structure in Classical Antiquity* (Cambridge: Cambridge University Press, 1992). He has excavated extensively in Greece and Britain.

**Walter C. Neale** was a student of Polanyi's at Columbia University in the late 1940s and later a member of the Interdisciplinary Project during the 1950s, contributing two papers to *Trade and Market in the Early Empires*. His books include *Economic Change in Rural India: Land Tenure and Reform in Uttar Pradesh, 1880-1955* (New Haven: Yale University Press, 1962), *Monies in Societies* (San Francisco: Chandler, 1976), and *Developing Rural India: Policies, Politics, and Progress* (Riverdale, MD: Riverdale Co.; Bombay: Allied Publishers, 1990). Neale is professor emeritus of economics at the University of Tennessee, Knoxville, and former chair of the Asian Studies Program.

**Vernon L. Scarborough** is associate professor in the Department of Anthropology at the University of Cincinnati. His latest articles have appeared in *La Recherche, Research in Economic Anthropology, Science,* and *The Sciences*. He is co-editor (with David R. Wilcox) of *The Mesoamerican Ballgame* (Tucson: University of Arizona, 1991). He has taught and carried out field work at the University of Texas at El Paso, the University of Khartoum, Sudan, and the University of Peshewar, Pakistan, and has worked extensively in Belize, and also in Guatemala and the Southwest United States.

**William Schaniel**, associate professor of economics at West Georgia College in Carrollton, Georgia, specializes in economic anthropology. His articles have appeared in the *Journal of Economic Issues* and *Studies in the Social Sciences*.

**David W. Tandy** is associate professor of classics and chair of the Interdisciplinary Program in Ancient Mediterranean Civilizations at the University of Tennessee, Knoxville. His articles focus on the economic and social history of early Greece.

# Introduction

## Colin A.M. Duncan and David W. Tandy

Karl Polanyi is justly famous for *The Great Transformation*,[1] his original and penetrating analysis of the socio-political implications of an economy integrated as a sole system of self-regulating markets. This work is usually remembered for its vivid descriptions of the intense disruption caused by the attempts in the early nineteenth century to implement the system. If nothing else, *The Great Transformation*, completed in the early 1940s, has always earned him at least a certain kind of approving footnote.[2] These encomia come his way because of the questions he raised and the way in which he raised them. How and why did the market shift from being simply one among many benign economic institutions to becoming, in its self-regulating form, the malignant devourer of almost all the other ones?

Polanyi emphasized the very novelty of the "market system" as a potent cause of turmoil, but it is also the case that 1) he knew that countless previous societies had contained markets in particular goods, and 2) he believed that human beings had not changed throughout the ages. Such belief in the fundamental consistency of human nature and behaviour over many centuries of civilization was very rare by the late 1930s. Nonetheless, it is clear from much of *The Great Transformation* that the outbreak of the war can hardly have taken Polanyi by surprise. World War II must have seemed to him to be a predictable and awful unravelling of all the positive trends he had grouped together under the rubric of "the great transformation." The war thus gave a certain poignancy to the American subtitle to the book (the main title in the case of the British edition), *The Political and Economic Origins of our Times*. We can scarcely gauge how disturbing the war was for him, but what we may ponder is

the seemingly abrupt abandonment of his critique of economism —
his own, highly distinctive parallel to Marx's nineteenth-century
critique of political economy. After the war, Polanyi turned from political economy to
anthropology. His intense interest in the nature of the human condition drove him to initiate an ambitious research project into all the various ways humans have historically integrated activities aimed at procuring the means of living into other social activities. In the spring of 1947, Polanyi joined the faculty at Columbia University in New York and in the following year he began to assemble the Interdisciplinary Project. Faculty and graduate students from Columbia and other institutions gathered for regular seminars, the final result of which was a volume of papers, *Trade and Market in the Early Empires*.[3] It proved to be an auspicious debut for this first generation of students, who carried out fundamental research on many parts of the world for many different periods of history. Polanyi himself moved on to other concerns; the increasing role of technology in contemporary society became the main focus of his attention until his death in Canada in 1964.

Almost four decades have passed now since *Trade and Market*. It has become clear in the last decade that another generation of scholars is carrying forth the project, albeit in a more extended manner. We have gathered in this volume papers from recent meetings of the Karl Polanyi Institute of Political Economy which amply demonstrate the breadth of Polanyi's influence across many disciplines.

It is unquestionable that *The Great Transformation* is the work for which Polanyi is best known. For all its notoriety among both admirers and detractors, its theoretical core has been less well digested than its historical narrative and vivid depictions. *Trade and Market*, by contrast, has proven theoretically fecund and we would like to turn now to an explanation of this. For this purpose we can use Kenneth Pike's celebrated distinction between the "emic" and "etic" interpretations of societies. In the former, the perspective is that of an insider, a participant in the community's activities. The ethnographer's informants offer emic explanations for their world, explanations that are not necessarily easily comprehended by outsiders. In the etic circumstance, the interpreter is on the outside looking in, and the subsequent interpretation tends to suffer from this fact. But the difficulties arising in either case from the conflict between objectivity and subjectivity can be obviated by implementing an explicitly dual axis of inquiry.[4]

Polanyi was making the same point in a different way. This is very clear from the argument that arose in the wake of *Trade and Market* over the notion of economic "surplus." Harry Pearson and other Polanyi acolytes argued that a surplus cannot exist until, or unless, it is named by the actual holders of the surplus.[5] Opponents responded that such a position was unreasonable: "I can see a surplus."[6] A good example of the distinction can be gleaned from a brief analysis of the behaviour of the Trobriander *guya'u* (big man), who by various avenues can accumulate many "extra" yams, with which he can choose to do one of several things. He may exchange the yams externally, getting in return consumable goods that he may then distribute among his people; he may share his yams by throwing a feast, a ceremony that unifies the community's support for him; he may redistribute the yams to members of the community who, for any of a variety of reasons, cannot in any other acceptable manner be provided with nourishment; or — and this is the most common action — he may pile up his yams for the purpose of display. The yams inevitably rot in their specially designed, open-for-viewing "yam house."[7] Interpreters who tend to restrict their observations to etic principles see these yams as a surplus and wonder why they are allowed to rot instead of being put to some "good use." Interpreters who lean toward valuing emic testimony understand these yams as already having been put to good social use. By this display the *guya'u* can show the entire community that he has more yams than anyone else: he is the biggest man. There is no surplus.

It is therefore not hard to see why one of Polanyi's most constant concerns became combatting what he termed the "economic solipsism," that tendency to assume that because we do things a certain way today, it must be the only way to do them.[8] For example, if we observe in a society that some items are traded in a setting that looks like a market, it does not follow that what we see before us is a manifestation of a self-regulating market system (by which we mean a set of integrated price-setting markets covering all goods). In a sense, Polanyi was reminding us that there is always an inner perspective for which we have every reason to suspect will be overlooked by the etic observer but which is critical to understanding the actual nature of the observed economic activity. Of course, both this emic/etic distinction and the split over the economic solipsism are essentially inseparable from the argument between the "primitivists" and the "modernists."[9]

At least three of the papers in this collection from the most recent International Karl Polanyi Conference address this point. Makoto Maruyama takes a very well-documented and well-studied society, Tokugawa Japan, and finds within it a distinction in monetary practices that would not necessarily have been noted by a narrowly etic, macro-level investigator. By turning his anthropological microscope on the exchange of goods, services and monies within smaller village communities, Maruyama finds a richness of economic relations not at all susceptible to the conventional tools of economic analysis, which always presuppose a single coherent monetary system. A thorough grounding in Polanyi's approach guided him to find an insightful way to marshall these previously ignored or misunderstood phenomena.

Just as Maruyama went behind the medieval Japanese veneer to find some fascinating arrangements, so Rhoda Halperin has literally situated herself within a community which itself resides inside a society generally regarded as the most completely marketized on the planet. It was because of her interaction with households practising alternative livelihood strategies that she was able to observe the microeconomic lives of people living in the interstices of a highly commodified world. Again, while she discusses phenomena not directly treated by Polanyi, her exposure to his thought enabled her to carry out her analysis.

By contrast, Walter Donlan goes behind the scenes into a society which has left us few records — indeed, there are some who would say no records at all. He displays ingenuity in his attempt to actually join, as it were, Odysseus' band of companions as they experience their adventures throughout the Mediterranean in the aftermath of the Trojan War. Donlan seeks to understand the world of Odysseus from the inside and makes use of ethnographic materials on other band-societies to help us understand what life for the early Greeks looked like on the eve of the emergence of the West.

The three authors we have just discussed have been developing portraits of particular societies. There is in consequence an inevitably static quality to their analyses. Indeed, this was a characteristic of the Columbia Interdisciplinary Project and of *Trade and Market* because of its historical framework. It must be recalled that, by contrast, Polanyi's earlier work was very much process-oriented,[10] and several of the other papers in the present volume do concern themselves chiefly with processes of social change, indeed upheaval. Most notably, Walter C. Neale, himself a participant in the Interdisciplinary Project while a junior faculty member at Yale and a double contributor to *Trade and Market*,[11] looks at the double movement in India. He shows that a process of marketization can occur with its own dynamic even contrary to the legislating will of a liberal colonial administration and then subsequently of the self-styled socialist governments of post-independence India. The rather paradoxical result has been the emergence of a deeply commodified society within a social context predisposed to be hostile to an invasive market system.

One might suppose from our remarks about these papers that the Polanyi perspective predisposes one to a teleological perspective on the process of marketization. To the contrary, as Polanyi was at pains to show in *The Great Transformation*, the successful completion of a process of universal commodification is not inevitable. William Schaniel shows how the Maori of New Zealand were able to exploit, instead of suffer passively at the hands of, the marketization process put upon them by the British. Discussing a completely different encounter between a society and a marketization process, Ian Morris dramatically demonstrates the successful long-term resistance to marketization in classical Athens. John Adams reviews for us the successful management of external trade by the Athenian authorities in order to contain the deleterious forces that would have otherwise been unleashed upon the citizenry. Whereas it may be observed that in all these cases economic arrangements are modulated by non-market factors such as status, in Vernon Scarborough's paper on Mayan water management, we see that economic formations and relations can be dictated by nature itself.

In sum, we present three papers on ancient Greeks, perhaps Polanyi's favourite historical population, and one on Polanyi's approach to their civilization. Subsequently, we offer insights into the economic lives of Classic Mayans, Tokugawa Japanese, New Zealand Maori, pre- and post-independence Indians, and modern-day Kentuckians. This very range of cultures bears testimony to the breadth of Polanyi's influence and to the importance of the tools that he has left for us.

## Notes

1. Polanyi 1944.
2. For example, "immensely stimulating" (Hobsbawm 1968, 55).
3. Polanyi, Arensberg, and Pearson 1957. On the Interdisciplinary Project see Tandy and Neale in this volume; Morris in this volume.
4. See Pike 1967 (first published 1954). Harris (1968, 568–604) discusses all of this at length. Headland, Pike, and Harris 1990, bring certain aspects of the debate up to date.
5. Pearson 1957; Dalton 1960; 1963.
6. Harris 1959. It is interesting that Marvin Harris was as responsible as anyone else for transferring Pike's emic/etic distinction from linguistics to anthropology.
7. Malinowski 1921, 8–10.
8. Polanyi 1977, 14.
9. See further Cartledge 1983; Mayhew, Neale, and Tandy 1985; Tandy and Neale in this volume; Morris in this volume.
10. See Tandy and Neale in this volume.
11. Neale 1957a; 1957b.

## References

Cartledge, Paul. 1983. " 'Trade and Politics' Revisited: Archaic Greece." In *Trade in the Ancient Economy*, edited by Peter Garnsey, Keith Hopkins, and C.R. Whittaker, 1–15. Berkeley: University of California.
Dalton, George. 1960. "A Note of Clarification on Economic Surplus." *American Anthropologist* 62:483–90.
———. 1963. "Economic Surplus, Once Again." *American Anthropologist* 65:389–93.
Harris, Marvin. 1959. "The Economy Has No Surplus?" *American Anthropologist* 61:185–99.
———. 1968. *The Rise of Anthropological Theory*. New York: Thomas Y. Crowell.
Headland, Thomas N., Kenneth L. Pike, and Marvin Harris. 1990. *Emics and Etics: The Insider/Outsider Debate*. Newbury Park, CA: Sage Publications.
Hobsbawm, Eric. J. 1968. *Industry and Empire*. London: Weidenfeld and Nicholson. Cited from Penguin edition, Harmondsworth, 1969.
Malinowski, Bronislav. 1921. "The Primitive Economics of the Trobriand Islanders." *Economic Journal* 31:1–16.
Mayhew, Anne, Walter C. Neale, and David W. Tandy. 1985. "Markets in the Ancient Near East: A Challenge to Silver's Argument and Use of Evidence." *Journal of Economic History* 45:127–34.
Neale, Walter C. 1957a. "Reciprocity and Redistribution in the Indian Village: Sequel to Some Notable Discussions." In Polanyi, Arensberg, and Pearson 1957, 218–36.

———. 1957b. "The Market in Theory and History." In Polanyi, Arensberg, and Pearson 1957, 357–72.
Pearson, Harry W. 1957b. "The Economy Has No Surplus: Critique of a Theory of Development." In Polanyi, Arensberg, and Pearson 1957, 320–41.
Pike, Kenneth. 1967. *Language in Relation to a Unified Theory of the Structure of Human Behavior.* 2d rev. ed. The Hague: Mouton.
Polanyi, Karl. 1944. *The Great Transformation.* New York: Holt Rinehart and Winston.
———. 1977. *The Livelihood of Man,* edited by Harry W. Pearson. New York: Academic Press.
Polanyi, Karl, Conrad M. Arensberg, and Harry W. Pearson, eds. 1957. *Trade and Market in the Early Empires.* Glencoe, IL: Free Press.

# 1

# Karl Polanyi's Distinctive Approach to Social Analysis and the Case of Ancient Greece: Ideas, Criticisms, Consequences*

## David W. Tandy and Walter C. Neale

Karl Polanyi's impact on the study of economic arrangements in ancient Greece owes far more to three of his general ideas — the idea of embeddedness, forms of integration, and the port of trade — than it does to his specific analyses of Greek materials. While, as it will become apparent in our discussion, there are reasons to have strong reservations about some of Polanyi's work on ancient Greece, he has made a positive contribution with his emphasis on the economy as an "instituted" process in which tightly-woven fabrics of socially prescribed activities govern the provision (making, moving, storage, and use) of material means. In arguing against applying the "market mentality" of the nineteenth and twentieth centuries to economies of antiquity, Polanyi has made it possible to discuss the issues without raising the misapprehensions and emotions associated with the words "modern" and "primitive"[1] — as our discussion of several works will make clear.

In our assessment of Polanyi's influence in the fields of ancient history and classics, we will repeatedly mention the names and the

---

* *The first version of this paper was delivered in Milan at the third International Karl Polanyi Conference, in November 1990. Tandy would like to acknowledge the financial support of the University of Tennessee, Knoxville, specifically the Department of Classics, the College of Liberal Arts, and the Office of the Vice-Chancellor for Academic Affairs. Gratitude also goes to the National Endowment for the Humanities, from whom he received a travel grant.*

work of Moses Finley, Walter Donlan, James Redfield, and Ian Morris. These scholars, who have established major reputations in these fields and many others, have made major use of Polanyi's ideas.[2] Each has relied heavily on the idea of embeddedness and especially on the idea of reciprocity as a way of integrating economic activities. One of the editors of this volume, David Tandy, has found the idea of the port of trade which emerged from the Columbia Project, invaluable in organizing his analysis of change in eighth-century Greece.[3] Surprisingly, however, not one of these scholars of antiquity has made any use of Polanyi's attempts at direct analysis of the Greek economy.

Most of Polanyi's specific analyses of the Greek economy are to be found in *The Livelihood of Man*,[4] often presumed to be the "last word" because it was published posthumously. But the manuscript does not appear to have been worked on between 1951 and the time of Polanyi's death in 1964. We have discussed the unreliability of *Livelihood* elsewhere,[5] and would add now that Moses Finley made efforts to forestall its publication, although it is important to note that Finley's concerns about *Livelihood* were not based on disagreement so much as disappointment with the unfinished manuscript.[6]

In this paper we review Polanyi's impact,[7] specific and general, in a number of areas of study: ancient Mediterranean accounting techniques, as observed at Tyre and in Mycenaean Greece; the worlds of Homer and Hesiod; the rise of the market in archaic Greece; Aristotelian economic analysis; and the ancient Greek ports of trade, especially fourth-century Naukratis.[8]

### On Style and Tone

It was some time before Polanyi's efforts garnered responses, positive or negative, from scholars of antiquity. This delay, we will try to show, may be at least partly the result of his style and tone. He was often assertive to an extreme. Many of his interpretations appear as unqualified statements when such phrasings as "probable" or "more likely than" would have been more suitable for his audience. We will use the adjectives "polemical" and "didactic" to refer to this assertive, even positivist style.

*The Great Transformation*[9] addressed current issues about how our world came to be the way it is and how we should try to manage it. A certain assertiveness was to be expected. For some, it was both convincing and enjoyable. For others, it was outrageous. But it was not confusing. The same was true of his Commentary article, "Our Obsolete Market Mentality."[10]

In *The Great Transformation,* Polanyi's style and tone may be called polemical. Beginning with *Trade and Market in the Early Empires*,[11] the controversial culmination of the Columbia University Interdisciplinary Project overseen by Polanyi, what had been polemical became didactic and Polanyi's style remained so thereafter. Again, arguments about the plausible or the probable were stated as matters of fact. But the issues with which Polanyi was now dealing were no longer of general and immediate interest. In 1944 and thereafter, the concern about the role of governments and the fear of authoritarian states were, and still are, general and immediate. However strongly Assyriologists feel about the issues in their discipline, no one worries about what Assurbanipal will do next. Thus, in the case of study of the ancient world, the didactic is judged against an always-doubting scholarly background, not against a background of anxiety. An unsurprising consequence is a strong reluctance to build upon Polanyi's merely plausible or probable interpretations when they are presented as patent fact. To illustrate, we offer, anecdotally, two cases from the work that led to *Trade and Market*.

A first instance: Polanyi thought it likely that the word commonly translated from the cuneiform as "market" should be rendered instead by "gate," and he put the question to A.L. Oppenheim of the Oriental Institute at the University of Chicago. Oppenheim asked one of his graduate students, Ronald Sweet, to test the possibility by substituting "gate" for "market" in a large body of cuneiform translations to see if the substitution violated any of the other translation rules. Sweet reported back that it did not. Polanyi then proceeded with his analysis of the ancient Near East on the assumption that the events previously interpreted as happening in a market happened under public authority at the gates of ancient cities. Polanyi, through his consultations with Oppenheim and Sweet, had not established that the word did in fact mean "gate" — only that "gate" was as likely a translation as "market." Polanyi's further analysis of the economic systems of the ancient Near East persuaded some that "gate" was indeed to be preferred to "market" — but the correctness of the change had not been demonstrated. It had only been argued for — more persuasively to some, less persuasively to others. It should be noted that, when Polanyi asked Oppenheim to contribute a chapter on the matter to *Trade and Market*, Oppenheim initially declined, remarking to Polanyi, "You have almost persuaded me that you are right; but I have heard only your side of the argument. It is possible that others could convince me otherwise."[12]

A second instance: *tamkarum* had been translated as "merchant." Polanyi thought that much of the contents of the tablets found at Kanish on the Halys river was far more consistent with a view of the *tamkarum* as a "public trustee" (consul at a foreign centre for trade) than as what one would normally think of as a "merchant." Submitting this proposition to Oppenheim and receiving permission to proceed, Polanyi constructed a new interpretation of the role of the *tamkarum*. Having begun, "we submit ... that Babylonia ... possessed neither market places nor a functioning market system of any description,"[13] Polanyi introduced his concluding paragraph to the chapter with the qualifying "If our interpretation is borne out by the facts...."[14] But in the ten pages between these statements, the tone is didactic and rarely qualified. It is not surprising that over many years Neale's graduate students treated the chapter as a statement of "proven" fact, not as a probably better interpretation of the documentary evidence. Neither should it be surprising that others have been wary of using an interpretation presented so didactically. The unqualified, didactic tone is even stronger in Polanyi's position paper for the *City Invincible* conference at the Oriental Institute in 1958.[15] In this piece, Polanyi presents an interpretation of Mycenaean "submonetary" accounting and "staple finance" (discussed more fully in the next section). Again, there are the occasional questions, the occasional "if," "apparently," or "in all probability" (the last is never a sincere qualification), yet there are also passages such as this:

> "Money," it is suggested, should be defined as "fungible things in definite uses, namely payment, standard, and exchange," while "price" should be replaced by the broader term "equivalency," which transcends markets.[16]

No source is cited for the phrases in quotation marks, nor for the "it" who suggests. Indeed, the "it" is Polanyi and others in the ongoing seminar at Columbia University, and the phrases are those that were settled upon there after a year of discussions (1957-58).

A reader of his analysis of the accounting systems should therefore be forgiven for thinking that Polanyi was saying, "this is the way Egyptian finance worked, that is the way Mycenaean finance worked; this is what the eastern neighbours were doing, this is what people in Alalakh were doing." Polanyi's explanations of the systems are plausible; we find them so probable as to be convincing, but scholars today do not have the ancient manuals or textbooks for accountants that would allow us to say, without doubt or qualification, "these are the devices and uses that were in fact operative."

We suspect that it may be that these didactic, impersonal statements have made many scholars wary of accepting Polanyi's interpretations; and this may be why his potential contributions to the study of Mycenaean Greece have received less attention than they deserve. Many academic disciplines consider the "best" work to be that which is error-free — classics leans especially on this criterion.[17] Thus, when one adds the proposition that Polanyi's treatment of Aristotle most probably contained one major error (see below), and then notes his mistranslation of Greek *chrysos* as silver (the word means gold), the wariness is even more understandable.[18]

### Ancient Accounting and Commodity Transactions

We return to Polanyi's paper in *City Invincible*.[19] Polanyi argued that the Mycenaean Palace economies differed from the Temple organizations to the south (Egypt) and east (Alalakh, Babylon) in that they operated without money or staple finance. The argument, incompletely reported here, is clear, intriguing, and many of us find it convincing. The fixed "equivalencies" (a kind of monetization) of staple finance allow substitution of one kind of thing for another in budgeting and balancing and so "may act as an inducement for the substitution of one staple for another."[20] This makes it hard to maintain supplies at the centre, and there is no way to determine the changes in the burdens consequent upon a change in taxes. In second-millennium Mycenaean Greece, by contrast, assessments and deliveries of discrete commodities were made according to specific proportions: commodities delivered from many tributary communities to Pylos, a political and economic centre in southwestern Greece, are six in number and appear regularly in the proportion 7:7:2:3:1.5:150; at Knossos, at the centre of King Minos' thalassocracy on Crete, the proportions of four commodities are 5:3:2:4.[21] These examples of "proportional tribute" had already been observed by Ventris and Chadwick;[22] Polanyi's contribution here was to observe that these proportions indicate a "composite tax" that assured a balance of these commodities at the centre. The composite tax created staple liquidity at the centre without the uncertainties threatened by staple finance or monetization. It worked through the simple operational devices of bringing in and passing out; inventory control could be achieved without knowledge of totals and without arithmetic calculation.

These keen observations are typical of Polanyi. For all their abstractness they focus in a practical way on operations — the ratios are not necessarily a reflection of the relative scarcity of each commodity; they focus on how goods move, not on why; they focus on their movement, not on their production.[23] If we understand the way in which staple finance worked in the Near East — there is no certainty that we do — it is clear that Polanyi has shown that there is another possible mechanism (call it Mycenaean?) for the accounting of centralized and stored community wealth.[24]

Polanyi concentrated on the role of numbers even when they were absent, noting that we can better grasp the purpose of Mycenaean bookkeeping techniques by comparing the use of accounting mechanisms in use in pre-British India[25] and at ancient Tyre. The prophet Ezekiel reports that traders came to the market at Tyre with great varieties of goods and exchanged them without the aid of any general set of equivalencies.[26] Polanyi guessed that each trader reckoned an ad hoc exchange ratio that would allow him to surrender $X$ number of his goods for each $Y$ number of another's goods. The exchange is then completed when one party runs out of goods. This method of money-free exchange does not require the sort of bookkeeping that we would otherwise anticipate to be used because the proportions used are strictly operational, of no validity or even meaning, apart from the exchange itself.[27]

**Homer**

In Homeric studies Polanyi's influence is subtle but clear. To start, we may measure his importance by the popularity and influence of Moses Finley's *World of Odysseus*.[28] Finley took part in the early stages of the Columbia Interdisciplinary Project and was greatly influenced by Polanyi's emphasis on institutions. Why Finley did not contribute to *Trade and Market* is not completely clear, although disagreement with Polanyi seems in itself unlikely to be the complete explanation.[29] Finley was subsequently criticized for taking the poetry out of the epics and analyzing them merely as sociological documents;[30] had Polanyi known about it, it would no doubt have pleased him.

Borrowing from Malinowski, Mauss, and Thurnwald,[31] Polanyi argued that there are three forms or patterns of economic integration in all societies. These patterns — reciprocity, redistribution, and exchange — are manifest in societies in different specific ways, usually so embedded in concrete institutions that they are not perceived by the people in these communities as separately economic. Neal Smelser's[32] adaptation of Malinowski, Mauss, and Thurnwald's work to reciprocity, redistribution, mobilization, and market, was embraced by Manning Nash in his interpretation of *Primitive and Peasant Economic Systems*[33] and by S.N. Eisenstadt in his *Political Systems of Empires*.[34] But another adaptation of Polanyi's scheme became more important to the study of the Homeric world. Marshall Sahlins broke down reciprocity into subcategories of generalized, balanced, and negative reciprocity,[35] which in turn were tested on the epics by Walter Donlan.[36] Donlan found that the Homeric economy is in fact driven by institutions integrating these ideas; and the proposition that the Homeric world is coherent in terms of these institutions supports the claim that the world depicted in the Homeric epics is actual, and not just an amalgam of elements of social life drawn from diverse sources.[37] Polanyi's general contribution supports the proposition that oral poetry and the social institutions implicit in it must make sense to the audience;[38] in this specific case we can see that the Homeric poems can be understood as reliable commentaries on the eighth-century Greek world in which they were recited. Polanyi's forms of economic integration enrich our understanding of Homer's world.

To take a specific instance: a recent use of some of Polanyi's ideas has led finally to a laser-cut through the Gordian Knot of the Diomedes and Glaucus episode in the Iliad. The Greek Diomedes and the Lycian Glaucus, an ally of the Trojans, meet on the field of battle. In the preliminary exchange of boasting before they would fight to the death, they discover that they are hereditary *xeinoi* ("guest-friends"), and that Diomedes' position is superior to Glaucus'. At the conclusion of the verbal exchange the two warriors agree to exchange gifts.

> Then did Zeus the son of Cronus take Glaucus' wits away, for he exchanged armor with Diomedes son of Tydeus, giving gold for bronze, armor worth 100 oxen for armor worth nine oxen (*Il.* 6.234-236).

Scholars have for a long time been concerned with why Glaucus is criticized by the poet for "outgiving" his *xeinos*.[39] Working within the tradition of Mauss and Polanyi, Donlan[40] has argued — we are tempted to say "demonstrated once and for all" — that Glaucus' error in outgiving Diomedes is to be explained by an understanding of *xenia* as a specialized form of gift-giving — reciprocity — with special rules for who is to outgive whom. According to *xenia* rules, Glaucus was required to outgive Diomedes; in the excitement of the moment, however, Glaucus overdid it. The audience then understands Homer's remark about Zeus taking away Glaucus' wits.

**Hesiod**

In the posthumous and flawed *Livelihood of Man*, Polanyi devoted a brief chapter to "The Hesiodic Age: Tribal Decay and Peasant Livelihood."[41] Hesiod, who lived the constrained life of a peasant in eighth- and seventh-century Boeotia in eastern Greece, presents to us a very different world than what we find in Homer.

In *Works and Days* Hesiod speaks of the driving force of hunger and the necessities of thrift and of calculated generosity among neighbours. Probably because of his occasional uncritical inclination to perceive the disembedding of the economy in the transformation from *Gemeinschaft* to *Gesellschaft*, Polanyi erred in asserting that behind the shift from kin to neighbour lay the collapse of a tribal order. This would be in keeping, of course, with many of the ethnographic records of primitive communities beset by Western colonial activities. But let us be very clear on this point: Polanyi was not a nostalgia-prone, "world-we-have-lost" admirer of the noble savage; nothing could be farther from the truth.[42] Polanyi was simply (but not simple-mindedly) following the virtual consensus of classics and ancient history that the nomenclature of the political organization of many of the Greek city-states that first arose around 700 B.C. derived from pre-existing tribal orders. Unfortunately, this position has been undercut by recent arguments[43] that tend to require a revision of this assumption about the early Greek city. It now appears to have been the case that in most locations tribes did not pre-exist the city-state, but were an invention of the city-state's new leadership, who endowed the new political divisions of "tribes" with a specious antiquity in order to provide an apparent legitimacy to artificial and essentially unfair relations.

In addition, Polanyi uncharacteristically restrained himself in his description of Hesiod's world and the rise of the individual within it, for he stopped short of declaring outright what we suspect he had been thinking: that the "rise of the individual" in early Greece was in no way *voluntary*. Basing ourselves in Tandy's[44] analysis of Hesiod's world, we are confident in asserting that the reciprocal and redistributive mechanisms that were in place in the Homeric epics and Hesiod's earlier poem, the *Theogony*, had for the most part disappeared, replaced by market-driven arrangements. There is no central *entrepôt* for Hesiod's surplus production, and certainly there are no benefits, material or otherwise, going back out from the centre. The result is that now Hesiod must bring his goods to *outside* markets. Regardless of whether these were ports of trade on the Gulf of Corinth where prices were fixed, or one-time markets where gains were dependent only on successful transportation of goods, the rise of these markets in the eighth century appears to have generated the introduction of private property. Encumberability and alienability followed soon thereafter. Our observations[45] here are at odds with what Polanyi wrote in *Livelihood*, but we emphasize that the ideas underlying the observations owe their genesis to Polanyi's other writings. Thus, what one has is an amplification of Polanyi and an example of criticism of *Livelihood* rather than criticism of the essential ideas found in *The Great Transformation*, *Trade and Market*, and elsewhere in Polanyi's writings. Polanyi's critical tools are outliving his pronouncements.

**The Rise of the Market**

Before we leave the world of Homer and Hesiod, we should discuss the important contribution of James Redfield[46] to our understanding of the rise of the market in Greece in the archaic period (about 700-490). His reliance on Polanyi is clear from his succinct synopsis of the difference between reciprocity and market exchange in the world of Homer: "Gift-exchange, in which the transaction is in the service of the relation, is rationally preferred to market-exchange, in which the relation is entered into for the sake of the transaction."[47] Redfield goes on to articulate the increasing importance of trade in the acquisition of wealth, arguing against the traditional position that ancient wealth resided exclusively in land:

> "Capital accumulation" produced a tax base which enabled cities to maintain the infrastructure which sustained further profitable reinvestment. The cities needed their rich, and there was never enough land for wealth to

be based to any important degree on large landholding. The real money was in trade — not in the actual travelling and negotiating (which was left to lower strata) but in financing and managing the developing international market.[48]

The observation that there was a shift during the archaic period from wealth based on status to status based on wealth, has as its underpinning Polanyi's fundamental concept of the disembedding of the economy as a society moves from status to contract, from *Gemeinschaft* (but without tribes) to *Gesellschaft*.

### Polanyi Discovers Aristotle

Other than his comments on accounting in Mycenaean Greece, Polanyi's only published work specifically on Greece (until the appearance of *Livelihood*) was "Aristotle Discovers the Economy."[49] It is probable that Polanyi's reputation among scholars of ancient Greece was not enhanced by this chapter in *Trade and Market*. Be it said for Polanyi, he did not venture alone into his analysis, but drew heavily upon conversations with Moses Finley.

The lack of enthusiasm for this piece — although this lack is dissipating[50] — is probably rooted in the differences between Polanyi's primary interests and the primary interests of most classicists and, again, in Polanyi's didactic style. Polanyi's primary interest in all his work after the publication of *The Great Transformation* was to reinforce his proposition that people had rarely approved of or allowed socially-uncontrolled market prices: market-organized societies were rare and the economy was normally "submerged" in (or at least dominated by) other social institutions. In addition to the capitalism of our times, the only other market-dominated society in history appears to have been the Hellenistic world of the eastern Mediterranean in the third and second centuries B.C. (see below). In

"Aristotle Discovers the Economy" Polanyi argued — we paraphrase grossly — that even the great Aristotle failed to understand the market system because it was so new, so strange, and so repugnant to the morality of the culture of the *polis*. Polanyi's core focus was not on *Aristotle's* thought but on the thesis that Aristotle's *inability* to understand the market showed how unprecedented, how strange a market system was. Polanyi wrote "Aristotle *Discovers the Economy*"; classicists have read "*Aristotle* Discovers the Economy."

For instance, Scott Meikle has argued that Moses Finley erred in claiming that Aristotle never attempted an "analytical economics."[51] Late in his article, Meikle associates — but also explicitly differentiates — Polanyi's and Finley's positions.[52] While one can argue that Meikle did not engage Polanyi on precisely the point that Polanyi wished to make, Meikle did point out that Polanyi so emphasized the moral aspects of Aristotle's arguments that he overlooked other possible interpretations of *Aristotle's* argument. Meikle's argument, cast as an "Anti-Finley," is that the *Ethics* tries to solve the problem of how "proportionate reciprocity" can be achieved in the exchange of goods in a market.[53] What we find persuasive is Meikle's argument that Aristotle *was* wrestling with the problem of how prices are formed; Meikle is right that Polanyi does not appear to have grasped that Aristotle *did* deal with prices as a theoretical problem. (We are *not* persuaded that Aristotle would have solved his problem correctly if only he had had Marx's labour theory of value to hand.)[54]

"Small beer"[55] is how Meikle characterized what Polanyi called the "massive and significant formulations"[56] of Aristotle, "the philosopher of Gemeinschaft."[57] To Polanyi they were "massive and significant" because they should persuade us that, from the beginning, at the beginning, and according to Aristotle, the market was anti-social; they were "massive" because they stated a major point of all of Polanyi's work and "significant" because Aristotle has been so important to Western thought. But for a classical scholar interpreting Aristotle, they do not seem nearly so massive or significant. Those who find the corpus of Polanyi's work an important help in interpreting the ancient Greek world should read "Aristotle Discovers the Economy" as an application of Polanyi's central thesis to the transition from the *polis'* proportionate reciprocity to market prices, and not as an important contribution to an understanding of how and why Aristotle thought as he did.[58]

### The Greek Port of Trade

Polanyi and his Columbia associates have played a pivotal role in our continuing inquiry into the ancient port of trade, which was a "purely economic settlement through which exchanges between two societies of different types could be organized and controlled."[59] Trading at these ancient ports of trade "had a history and logic of its own, stemming from the principle of a politically neutral meeting place."[60] Without question, Polanyi's analysis of the port of trade is necessary to an understanding of the institutions — economic, social, and political — at the ports of trade that featured Greek involvement, such as Al Mina (the international *entrepôt* in northern Syria, probably controlled from Urartu), and Ezekiel's Tyre (controlled from Assur).

Herodotus' description of the routes required of incoming traders makes clear that the trade between Egypt and the outside world that took place in Naukratis, the port of trade set up on the Nile Delta by Greek traders in the last decade of the seventh century,[61] was what Polanyi called administered trade,[62] in this case administered with the objective of controlling the movements of goods into and out of the Egyptian empire.[63]

Polanyi's analysis[64] of the role of Kleomenes, Alexander's governor at Alexandria, is right on the mark, illustrating clearly the disruption to other places caused by Kleomenes' management of trade in the new "world market" in the eastern Mediterranean. During the 320s Kleomenes was able to direct shipments of grains out of Egypt through Naukratis and Rhodes to those places where the return was greatest. This activity caused hardship at Athens and other centres dependent on outside grain, and, to put it mildly, tarnished Kleomenes' subsequent reputation. Thanks mostly to the accounts of Arrian and Demosthenes,[65] Kleomenes has been unfairly painted as a villain who, upon his demise at the hands of Ptolemy Soter in 323, had accumulated in the Alexandrian treasury a surplus of 8,000 talents, indeed an enormous sum. But this sum, Polanyi asserted, is not to be understood as somehow a personal accumulation by Kleomenes, and therefore as evidence of his venality, but as a surplus from the careful administration of the grain trade by Kleomenes, to the benefit of the Egyptian economy, probably, Polanyi concluded confidently, to the benefit of the Egyptian farmers themselves.[66]

Polanyi's revisionist picture of Kleomenes runs counter to Michael Rostovtzeff's (long standard) analysis that this was a period that witnessed the triumph of *laissez-faire* principles: "after Alexander, [the grain trade] became free, once and for all."[67] Polanyi's revision has led one ancient historian to attack Polanyi's conclusions as a "Rostovtzeff-turned-on-his-head view of the Hellenistic world."[68] But this criticism is founded upon the modernist economic fallacy that Polanyi warned all historians against: the belief that the way *we* do things is the *natural* way to do things.[69] Rostovtzeff was caught in the solipsism;[70] others, equally unaware, were and still are also caught.[71]

### Summary

Polanyi's importance in the study of ancient Greece does not derive from his essays and chapters on Greece. Rather, his great contribution has been to recast issues earlier debated between "primitivists" and "modernists." He has opened new possibilities for analyses and interpretations — of how people organized their economic lives and how they conducted trade in the absence of a modern market system — *without* calling up the pejorative connotations of "primitive." He has also made it possible to use comparative materials from non-Western cultures, including ethnographic descriptions of non-literate societies, to broaden our understanding of early Greece — for, until the rise of the *polis* in the seventh and sixth centuries (coincident with the beginnings of the market), the early Greeks were not what we call "Western."

We can now see that the issues underlying the old debate between modernists and primitivists were arguments about whether economistic or sociological analyses are more appropriate. There is still room for discussion of the periods and respects in which one or the other might be more appropriate. (For example, many aspects of the economy of the eastern Mediterranean in the third and second centuries B.C. may well be made clearer by an application of market analysis.) Paul Cartledge,[72] in restating the old positions, now has argued persuasively that the burden resides squarely on the shoulders of more recent "modernizers" to try to make their case. This is just one of Karl Polanyi's many achievements; it has already led to important reinterpretations of ancient Greek economy and society, and it should and doubtless will lead to more.

### Notes

1. The great debate between the primitivists and the modernists goes back at least to the nineteenth-century confrontation between Karl Bücher with his *oikos* theory and Eduard Meyer, a leading modernist. The most important published pieces by the principals have been collected by Moses Finley (1979), who often discussed the controversy himself (see especially 1976/77; 1980, 42–49). For other discussions of the controversy, see Pearson 1957; Austin and Vidal-Naquet 1977, 3–7; Cartledge 1983.
2. The work of Finley, Donlan, and Redfield is discussed in the body of this paper. An excellent example of Ian Morris's work is the paper in this volume, but see also Morris 1986a; 1986b.
3. Tandy 1988; forthcoming, chapters 4 and 5.
4. Polanyi 1977.
5. Mayhew, Neale, and Tandy 1985.

6. The manuscript bears the date of May 1951 (Dalton 1981, 89, n. 1). Finley "begged" Ilona Ducyznska not to let *Livelihood* see print (Tandy, conversation with Finley, 1984) and he urged Harry Pearson not to use Polanyi's unpublished material on Greece in *Livelihood* (Neale, conversation with Finley, 1985).
7. It is not our intention to revise the important assessments of Karl Polanyi's work by Sally Humphreys, Yvon Garlan, and Lucette Valensi. The brief treatments by Garlan (1973) and Valensi (1974) emphasize the place of Polanyi's work in the fields of economic anthropology and economic history (and introduced Polanyi to many French-speaking scholars, who otherwise were not aware of Polanyi's importance), but neither is as broad and far-reaching as Humphreys's discussion of "History, Economics and Anthropology: The Work of Karl Polanyi" (1969), in which she discusses Polanyi's positions on i) money, markets, and trade; ii) economic theory; and iii) forms of economic integration (reciprocity, redistribution, householding, and market exchange). Humphreys offers valuable guidance in identifying Polanyi's role in the development of various disciplinary positions: for example, his influence on Popper and others on the importance within sociology of studying institutions rather than human nature. We have little to add to Humphreys' assessment of Polanyi's career, save to note that his influence or presence has increased in the twenty years since that assessment appeared, as is clear from Paul Cartledge's (1983) assessment of the influence of Hasebroek and Polanyi on recent work on the character of archaic trade.
8. There is available, in the archive of the Karl Polanyi Institute of Political Economy in Montréal, a manuscript entitled (for cataloguing purposes) *Greek Manuscript*. It was written by Polanyi after 1947, but apart from chapter titles and location (box 11), we (Tandy and Neale) know little else about it. Tandy has inspected (and shared with his colleagues, among them Walter Donlan — see his paper below) the first chapter, "Reciprocity and Redistribution in Homeric Greece," an insightful analysis of the Homeric world that suffers only from preceding the decipherment of Linear B and from employing outdated sociological assumptions. The other chapters are "The Hesiodic Age: Tribal Decay," "The Solonic Crisis," "Peisistratus: The Tyrannis Episode," "Polis and Agora," "Local Markets and Overseas Trade," "Securing Grain Imports," and "The Growth of Market Trade." Much of this material probably bears some kinship to the 1951 manuscript that saw print posthumously as *The Livelihood of Man* (Polanyi 1977) and many of the titles correspond with topics of his lectures at Columbia University.
9. Polanyi 1944.
10. Polanyi 1947. Those familiar with Polanyi's earlier writings would know whether the same was true of these writings.
11. Polanyi, Arensberg, and Pearson 1957.
12. Neale's memory of the discussion at a meeting of the group during spring 1955. A more formal version of the exchange is given in Polanyi 1957a, 17. The chapter, "A Bird's-Eye View of Mesopotamian Economic History," that Oppenheim did contribute to *Trade and Market* was a substitute for the chapter that

Polanyi would have liked to have included in the volume. Tandy concedes that this explanation of Oppenheim's hesitation to contribute more fully undermines his arguments that Finley had reasons more compelling than disagreement for not contributing to *Trade and Market* (below, n. 29). It also raises another, probably more interesting irony: that Oppenheim and Finley, Polanyi's most prominent mentors on Mesopotamia and Greece respectively, declined to commit themselves fully to Polanyi's programme.
13. Polanyi 1957a, 16.
14. Polanyi 1957a, 26.
15. Polanyi 1960.
16. Polanyi 1960, 341.
17. Redfield 1991, 6.
18. In fact, the only immediate response we have found to Polanyi's contribution to *City Invincible* is in a brief review that concluded with special reference to this error as "Polanyi's howler on page 342" (Jones 1962, 62). It strikes us as a simple enough mistake to make, and essentially pointless to dwell on.
19. Polanyi 1960.
20. Polanyi 1960, 343.
21. These records were made using a script known as Linear B, which represented an early form of the Greek language and which was the sixteenth-century successor to Linear A, which had been used previously and which is not Greek.
22. Ventris and Chadwick 1973 [1956], 290ff., 302–303.
23. On this last distinction, see below, n. 69.
24. The observations are typical in another way: While we have seen no scholarship gainsaying him, we have found no scholarship in the subsequent quarter century acknowledging that he ever made these specific observations. Polanyi does not appear to figure in the mainstream of "economic" analyses of Mycenaean Greece until the work of J. T. Killen, whose important article on the Mycenaean economy reveals both the general value of Polanyi's substantive position for the study of Mycenaean Greece and the specific utility of Polanyi's theory of proportional tribute (Killen 1988).
25. See Neale 1957.
26. Ezekiel 27.
27. Polanyi 1960, 343–45.
28. Finley 1954; 1965; 1978.
29. Humphreys (1969, 42–43) believes that Finley did not contribute because of disagreement; however, he appears to have been asked repeatedly to contribute (Neale, personal recollection). Finley did indeed distance himself from Polanyi's positions (Finley 1975, 117), but there is no ignoring Finley's use of Polanyi's forms of integration in *The World of Odysseus*, and the profound appreciation expressed by Finley in the original and the two revisions of *The World of Odysseus* (1954, 156; 1965, xvi; 1978, 11). (Finley remained a close friend of Polanyi's widow, Ilona Ducyznska, until her death in 1978.) Finley's trouble with Senator McCarran's Internal Security Subcommittee, which eventually led to his dismissal from Rutgers University in 1952 (Schrecker 1986, 171–179), may have discouraged him from contributing to *Trade and Market*. Also, he left

the Project when offered a position at Oxford in the fall of 1954. (In Winter 1955 he went on to Cambridge, where he remained until his death in 1986. Most of the papers that appeared in *Trade and Market* were written no earlier than 1954–55.)
30. Finley 1978, 142.
31. Malinowski 1922; Mauss 1925; Thurnwald 1932.
32. Smelser 1958/59.
33. Nash 1966; cf. Nash 1959.
34. Eisenstadt 1963.
35. Sahlins 1965, 147–49; 1972, 193–96; also 1968, 82–86; cf. Service 1966, 14–21; 1979, 16–22.
36. Donlan 1982.
37. Anthony Snodgrass (1974, 118) concludes that Homeric society reflects "a mixture of practices, derived from a diversity of historical sources." Earlier Snodgrass (1971, 389) suggested that epic society was an "artificial amalgam of widely separated historical stages." But see A. G. Geddes, on Snodgrass 1974: "Not all his readers, however, will be convinced that, for example, the use of the plough is incompatible with the transmission of property among the kin of one sex" (Geddes 1984, 19). Adkins (1972a, 10; cf. 1960, chapters 1–3; 1963; 1971; 1972b) argues for a consistency of values in the Homeric poems; *contra:* A. A. Long finds no "consistent pattern of society" (Long 1970, 137, n. 58). But other types of consistency are observable. Whitman (1958, 87–101) long ago argued the aesthetic similarities between Homeric epic and eighth-century (Geometric) vase decoration. Onians (1951, esp. chapter 1) argued that the physiognomy of the heroes is Geometric.
38. "Since [Homer] is telling his story to an audience, the meaning he conveys must be a meaning *to them*" (Redfield 1975, 23; emphasis original); compare Rose, for whom the epics contain "a picture of social, political, and economic relationships familiar to the poet and his audience" (1975, 131).
39. All the ancient material and modern scholarship is collected in Calder 1984.
40. Donlan 1989.
41. Polanyi 1977, 147–57. This is probably essentially identical to the chapter of the *Greek Manuscript* (see above, n. 8).
42. Polanyi on the generosity of the individual within a tribe: "The premium set on generosity is so great when measured in terms of social prestige as to make any other behavior than that of self-forgetfulness simply not pay" (1944, 46).
43. Bourriot 1976; Roussel 1976; Donlan 1985.
44. Tandy 1988.
45. Tandy 1988.
46. Redfield 1986.
47. Redfield 1986, 37. Redfield nowhere explicitly acknowledges Polanyi's influence, but personal conversations with Tandy and this quotation make the intellectual debt clear. In fact, it was Redfield who introduced Tandy to Polanyi's work.
48. Redfield 1986, 48.
49. Polanyi 1957b.

50. Morris 1993, in this volume.
51. Meikle 1979; Meikle 1991a works from this, he says, but the points made are different. A summary statement of Meikle's criticism is at 1979, 64.
52. Meikle 1979, 71–73; cf. 1991a, 178–79.
53. Aristotle's "answer is that it is done by establishing the proportionate *equality* between the products .... [If] the exchange [is] transacted on that basis, then the requirement of proportionate *reciprocity* will have been achieved ...." To explain "justice in exchange as 'proportionate *reciprocity*' ... depends on explaining what 'proportionate *equality* between products' means. It is the ramifications of this problem that absorb and bewilder Aristotle in the two-thirds of the chapter that still remain" (Meikle 1979, 59; emphasis original. Cf. 1991a, 158–59). Compare this last sentence with Polanyi (1957b, 66): "according to Aristotle ... prices should conform to the rules of justice *(the actual formulation remaining quite obscure)*" (Polanyi 1957b, 66; emphasis added).
54. See further Meikle 1991b.
55. Meikle 1979, 72; 1991a, 180.
56. Polanyi 1957b, 79.
57. Polanyi 1957b, 88.
58. Morris' essay in this volume emphasizes the importance of the Aristotle piece to understanding Polanyi's substantivism.
59. Austin and Vidal-Naquet 1977, 66–68.
60. Revere 1957, 51.
61. Austin 1970.
62. Polanyi 1957a; 1977, 94–95.
63. Austin does not mention Polanyi in his monograph on Greeks in Egypt — although it is based on his dissertation written under Moses Finley — but Austin does make it clear in his later reader (Austin and Vidal-Naquet 1977) how important Polanyi's concept is to understanding Naukratis.
64. Polanyi 1977, 240–51.
65. It is Diodorus (18.14.1) who reports that Ptolemy found 8,000 talents when he took over Alexandria, presumably from Kleomenes. Demosthenes (56.7) tells us that Kleomenes harmed the Athenians by driving up the price of grain. Arrian (7.23.6) reports, without further elaboration, that Kleomenes was "an evil man who had done many evil things in Egypt." Pseudo-Aristotle (*Economics* 1352a17–1352b25) relates at length some sharp dealings by Kleomenes, but none imply personal gain. Tarn, however, transforms Diodorus' neutral statement into: "[Kleomenes] amassed 8,000 talents *by his misdeeds*, a fantastic sum at a time when the richest man in Greece was perhaps worth 160 talents; even Harpalus, with Alexander's treasure at command, only *managed to steal* 5,000 talents" (Tarn 1948, 129; emphases added). Another modern scholar speaks of Kleomenes "making himself a fortune stated to amount to 8,000 talents" (Hammond 1967, 634). The talents in the treasury were not Kleomenes' personal hoard and were the result of aggressive administration, perhaps of some sharp doing, but not of misdoing.
66. Polanyi 1977, 248.

67. Rostovtzeff 1930, 575 (by "after Alexander," who died in 323, Rostovtzeff means "after 330"). Polanyi appears generally to have respected and even depended on the work of Rostovtzeff, but this statement is pointedly quoted by Polanyi (1977, 239) as erroneous.
68. Figueira 1984, 29. This is really rather poignant when one considers Marx's assertion in the afterword of the second German edition of *Capital* that in Hegel's hands dialectic "is standing on its head *(auf dem Kopf)*" (Marx 1967, 20). There are those among us who believe that it is Rostovtzeff and his blindered followers who need their heads righted. Figueira concludes his criticism of Polanyi by accusing him of "primitivizing" (p. 30).
69. Johannes Hasebroek (1933) and Moses Finley, in one of Finley's earliest publications (Finkelstein 1935, 320), anticipated Polanyi's position on the economic solipsism by arguing strongly against the use of modern economic terms such as "firm" and "capitalism." Polanyi's most succinct treatment of the fallacy is 1977, 14–17; cf. Mayhew, Neale, and Tandy 1985, 129. Marx had of course worked through much of this in his analysis of pre-capitalist formations in the *Grundrisse* (Marx 1973, 471–514; Hobsbawm 1964), which was not readily available until 1953. While on the subject, it is fair to point out that Polanyi has been criticized, by Marxists mostly, for failing to acknowledge the notion of exploitation and for emphasizing "patterns of allocation rather than relations of production" (Cartledge 1983, 6); Godelier (1981), however, defends Polanyi on this particular point.
70. As Meyer Reinhold (1946) showed, with his subject's own approval; see also Ranowisc 1961; Frank 1975; Finley 1980, 53.
71. Figueira is often quite correct in calling Polanyi to task for overstating (for polemical or didactic purposes) certain of his positions. But his criticisms fall flat by being too dependent on the posthumous *Livelihood* (Polanyi 1977: see above, with n. 6) — and too unaware of important distinctions that Polanyi emphasized. For example, price-making markets may have existed from an early date and so we can talk about them, but Polanyi was concerned with how *most* people gained their livelihoods, not whether peripheral price-making markets were present or absent. *Most* people before the fourth century did not depend on markets for the acquisition of food, clothing, and shelter; they acquired their livelihoods through other mechanisms.
72. Cartledge 1983.

## References

Adkins, Arthur. 1960. *Merit and Responsibility: A Study in Greek Values*. Oxford: Oxford University Press.

———. 1963. "'Friendship' and 'Self-Sufficiency' in Homer and Aristotle." *Classical Quarterly* 13:30–45.

———. 1971. "Homeric Values and Homeric Society." *Journal of Hellenic Studies* 91:1–14.
———. 1972a. *Moral Values and Political Behaviour in Ancient Greece*. London: Chatto and Windus.
———. 1972b. "Homeric Gods and the Values of Homeric Society." *Journal of Hellenic Studies* 92:1–19.
Austin, Michel M. 1970. *Greece and Egypt in the Archaic Age*. Cambridge: Cambridge Philological Society.
Austin, Michel M., and Pierre Vidal-Naquet. 1977. *Economic and Social History of Ancient Greece: An Introduction*. Berkeley: University of California Press.
Bourriot, Felix. 1976. *Recherches sur la nature du génos: étude d'histoire sociale athénienne. Périodes archaïque et classique*. Paris: H. Champion.
Calder, William M., III. 1984. "Gold for Bronze: *Iliad* 6.232-236." In *Studies Presented to Sterling Dow on the Occasion of His Eightieth Birthday*, 31–35. Durham, NC: Duke University Press.
Cartledge, Paul. 1983. "'Trade and Politics' Revisited: Archaic Greece." In *Trade in the Ancient Economy*, edited by Peter Garnsey, Keith Hopkins, and C. R. Whittaker, 1–15. Berkeley: University of California Press.
Dalton, George. 1981. "Comment." *Research in Economic Anthropology* 4:69–93.
Donlan, Walter. 1982. "Reciprocities in Homer." *Classical World* 75:137–75.
———. 1985. "The Social Groups of Dark Age Greece." *Classical Philology* 80:293–308.
———. 1989. "The Unequal Exchange between Glaucus and Diomedes in Light of the Homeric Gift-Economy." *Phoenix* 43.1:1–15.
Eisenstadt, S. N. 1963. *The Political Systems of Empires*. Glencoe, IL: Free Press.
Figueira, Thomas J. 1984. "Karl Polanyi and Ancient Greek Trade: The Port of Trade." *The Ancient World* 10:15–30.
Finkelstein (Finley), M. I. 1935. "*Emporos, Naukleros* and *Kapelos*: A Prolegomena to the Study of Athenian Trade." *Classical Philology* 30:320–36.
Finley, Moses I. 1954. *The World of Odysseus*. New York: Viking.
———. 1957/58. "Mycenaean Palace Archives and Economic History." *Economic History Review*, 2d ser., 10:128–41.
———. 1965. *The World of Odysseus*. Rev. ed. New York: Viking.
———. 1975. *The Use and Abuse of History*. New York: Viking.
———. 1976/77. "The Ancient City from Fustel de Coulanges to Max Weber and Beyond." *Comparative Studies in Society and History* 19:305–27.
———. 1978. *The World of Odysseus*. 2d rev. ed. New York: Viking.
———, ed. 1979. *The Bücher-Meyer Controversy*. New York: Arno.
———. 1980. *Ancient Slavery and Modern Ideology*. London: Chatto and Windus. Cited from Penguin edition (New York, 1983).
Frank, R. I. 1975. "Marxism and Ancient History." *Arethusa* 8.1:43–58.
Garlan, Yvon. 1973. "L'oeuvre de Polanyi: la place de l'économie dans les sociétés." *La Pensée* 171:118–27.
Geddes, A. G. 1984. "Who's Who in 'Homeric' Society?" *Classical Quarterly* 34:17–36.
Godelier, M. 1981. "Discussion." *Research in Economic Anthropology* 4:64–69.
Hammond, N. G. L. 1967. *A History of Greece to 322 B.C.* 2nd ed. Oxford: Oxford University Press.

Hasebroek, Johannes. 1933. *Trade and Politics in Ancient Greece.* Translated by L. M. Fraser and D. C. MacGregor. London: G. Bell and Sons. Reprinted Chicago: Ares, 1976.

Hobsbawm, E. J., ed. 1964. *Karl Marx: Pre-Capitalist Economic Formations.* Translated by Jack Cohen. London: Lawrence and Wishart.

Humphreys, S. C. 1969. "History, Economics, and Anthropology: The Work of Karl Polanyi." *History and Theory* 8:165–212. Reprinted and cited from her *Anthropology and the Greeks.* London: Routledge and Kegan Paul, 1978.

Jones, T. B. 1962. Review of *City Invincible* (see Polanyi 1960). *Archaeology* 15:61–62.

Killen, J. T. 1988. "The Linear B Tablets and the Mycenaean Economy." In *Linear B: A 1984 Survey,* edited by Anna Morpurgo-Davies and Yves Duhoux, 241–305. Louvain-la-Neuve: Peeters.

Long, A. A. 1970. "Morals and Values in Homer." *Journal of Hellenic Studies* 90:121–139.

Malinowski, B. 1922. *Argonauts of the Western Pacific.* London: Routledge and Kegan Paul.

Marx, Karl. 1967. *Capital.* Translated by Samuel Moore and Edward Aveling. New York: International Publishers.

———. 1973. *Grundrisse.* Translated by M. Nicolaus. New York: Vintage.

Mauss, Marcel. 1925. *The Gift.* Translated by Ian Cunnison. New York: Norton, 1967.

Mayhew, Anne, Walter C. Neale, and David W. Tandy. 1985. "Markets in the Ancient Near East: A Challenge to Silver's Argument and Use of Evidence." *Journal of Economic History* 45:127–134.

Meikle, Scott. 1979. "Aristotle and the Political Economy of the Polis." *Journal of Hellenic Studies* 99:57–73.

———. 1991a. "Aristotle and Exchange Value." In *A Companion to Aristotle's Politics,* edited by David Keyt and Fred D. Miller, Jr., 156–81. Oxford: Oxford University Press.

———. 1991b. "Aristotle on Equality and Market Exchange." *Journal of Hellenic Studies* 111:193–96.

Meyer, Eduard. 1895. *Die wirtschaftliche Entwicklung des Altertums.* Cited from his *Kleine Schriften,* 2d ed. Vol. 1, 79–168. Halle: M. Niemeyer, 1924. Reprinted also in Finley 1979a.

Morris, I. 1986a. "Gift and Commodity in Archaic Greece." *Man* 21:1–17.

———. 1986b. "The Use and Abuse of Homer." *Classical Antiquity* 5:81–138.

Nash, Manning. 1959. "Some Social and Cultural Characteristics of Economic Development." *Economic Development and Cultural Change* 7:137–50.

———. 1966. *Primitive and Peasant Economic Systems.* San Francisco: Chandler.

Neale, Walter C. 1957. "Reciprocity and Redistribution in the Indian Village." In Polanyi, Arensberg, and Pearson 1957, 218–35.

Onians, R. B. 1951. *The Origins of European Thought about the Body, the Mind, the Soul, the World, Time, and Fate.* Cambridge: Cambridge University Press.

Oppenheim, A. Leo. 1957. "A Bird's-Eye View of Mesopotamian Economic History." In Polanyi, Arensberg, and Pearson 1957, 27–37.

Pearson, Harry W. 1957. "The Secular Debate on Economic Primitivism." In Polanyi, Arensberg, and Pearson 1957, 3–11.

Polanyi, Karl. 1944. *The Great Transformation.* New York: Holt Rinehart and Winston.
———. 1947. "Our Obsolete Market Mentality." *Commentary* 3:109–17.
———. 1957a. "Marketless Trading in Hammurabi's Time." In Polanyi, Arensberg, and Pearson 1957, 12–26.
———. 1957b. "Aristotle Discovers the Economy." In Polanyi, Arensberg, and Pearson 1957, 64–94.
———. 1960. "On the Comparative Treatment of Economic Institutions in Antiquity with Illustrations from Athens, Mycenae, and Alalakh." In *City Invincible,* edited by C. H. Kraeling and R. M. Adams, 329–50. Chicago: University of Chicago Press.
———. 1977. *The Livelihood of Man,* edited by Harry W. Pearson. New York: Academic Press. Edited from the manuscript dated May 1951 and from lectures delivered at Columbia, 1947–53.
Polanyi, Karl, Conrad M. Arensberg, and Harry W. Pearson, eds. 1957. *Trade and Market in the Early Empires.* Glencoe, IL: Free Press.
Ranowisc, A. B. 1961. Review of Rostovtzeff 1941. In his *Aufsätze zur alten Geschichte.* Translated by G. von Bockisch, 56–74. Berlin: Akademie-Verlag.
Redfield, James M. 1975. *Nature and Culture in the Iliad: The Tragedy of Hector.* Chicago: University of Chicago Press.
———. 1986. "The Development of the Market in Archaic Greece." In *The Market in History,* edited by B. L. Anderson and A. J. H. Latham, 29–58. London: Croom Helm.
———. 1991. "Classics and Anthropology." *Arion,* n.s., 1.2:5–23.
Reinhold, Meyer. 1946. "Historian of the Classical World: Critique of Rostovtzeff." *Science and Society* 10:361–91.
Revere, R. B. 1973. "'No Man's Coast': Ports of Trade in the Eastern Mediterranean." In Polanyi, Arensberg, and Pearson 1957, 38–63.
Rose, Peter W. 1975. "Class Ambivalence in the *Odyssey.*" *Historia* 24:129–49.
Rostovtzeff, Michael. 1930. "The Corn-Trade and the Spartocids in Hellenistic Times." In *The Cambridge Ancient History,* Vol. 7, edited by S. A. Cook, F. E. Adcock, and M. P. Charlesworth, 574–82. Cambridge: Cambridge University Press.
———. 1941. *The Social and Economic History of the Hellenistic World.* Oxford: Oxford University Press.
Roussel, Denis. 1976. *Tribu et cité: études sur les groupes sociaux dans les cités grecques aux époques archaïque et classique.* Paris: Les Belles Lettres.
Sahlins, Marshall D. 1965. "On the Sociology of Primitive Exchange." In *The Relevance of Models for Social Anthropology,* edited by M. Gluckman and F. Eggan, 139–236. London: Tavistock.
———. 1968. *Tribesmen.* Englewood Cliffs, NJ: Prentice-Hall.
———. 1972. *Stone Age Economics.* Chicago: Aldine.
Schrecker, E. W. 1986. *No Ivory Tower.* New York and Oxford: Oxford University Press.
Service, E. 1966. *The Hunters.* Englewood Cliffs, NJ: Prentice-Hall.
———. 1979. *The Hunters.* 2d ed. Englewood Cliffs, NJ: Prentice-Hall.
Smelser, Neil J. 1958/59. "A Comparative Review of Exchange Systems." Review of *Trade and Market. Economic Development and Cultural Change* 7:173–82.

Snodgrass, Anthony M. 1971. *The Dark Age of Greece*. Edinburgh: Edinburgh University Press.
———. 1974. "An Historical Homeric Society?" *Journal of Hellenic Studies* 94:114–25.
Tandy, David W. 1988. "Never Any Good:" Changing Forms of Economic Integration in Hesiod's World. Montréal: Karl Polanyi Institute.
———. Forthcoming. *The Destruction of the Market in Early Greece*. Unpublished manuscript.
Tarn, W. W. 1948. *Alexander the Great*. Cambridge: Cambridge University Press.
Thurnwald, R. 1932. *Economics in Primitive Communities*. London: Oxford University Press.
Valensi, L. 1974. "Anthropologie économique de Karl Polanyi." *Annales: économies, sociétés, civilisations* 29:1311–19. Translated by Ludgard De Decker and Gregory Blue in *Research in Economic Anthropology* 4 (1981):3–12.
Ventris, Michael, and John Chadwick. 1973 [1956]. *Documents in Mycenaean Greek*. 2d ed. Cambridge: Cambridge University Press.
Whitman, C. H. 1958. *Homer and the Heroic Tradition*. Cambridge, MA: Harvard University Press.

# 2

# Chief and Followers in Pre-State Greece*

## Walter Donlan

As Karl Polanyi knew, Greece just before the city-state is the best documented early-historical example of the embedded economy. In books 9-12 of the *Odyssey*, we are given a rare, animated glimpse into the positive and negative effects of such a system. In these key books we observe Odysseus and his "companions" (*hetairoi*) on their way home from the Trojan War, as told by Homer and narrated by Odysseus himself. Although their adventures take place in a fantasy world, the sociological content of the stories closely reproduces the kinds of relationships between a leader and his followers observed by ethnographers of ranked societies led by big men or low-level chiefs. The rules, norms and behaviours among the community of raiding warriors reflect explicitly or implicitly the value system and the economic, social and political institutions of the village communities in which these men lived.

Before I analyze the Homeric text in detail, let me set the historical and ethnographical stage.[1] The pre-state or state-formative period in Greece dates from approximately 850 to about 750 B.C., roughly the last century of the long Dark Age, so called, which began with the final collapse of the Late Bronze Age kingdoms around 1150 or 1100. Most of the people of that sparsely populated era lived in hamlets and villages of a few dozen to several hundred inhabitants; there were also a select few village clusters on the mainland that formed small towns with populations perhaps in the low

---

* *The original version of this paper was delivered at the fourth International Karl Polanyi Conference, held in Montréal in November 1992.*

thousands. In the Homeric epics, which reflect the society of the pre-state period, these little villages are called *polis* or *astu*, the same names given to the much larger towns and cities of later Greece. The individual settlements were pretty much self-sufficient economically and were more or less politically autonomous, but were also parts of a larger entity, the *demos*, a word which signified then, as later, both the "people" as an ethnic group and the tribal territory they occupied. A *demos* might consist of a single village and its farmlands and pastures; more typically, however, the *demos* contained a central *polis* and one or more lesser settlements. Politically, the village communities were headed by a chief, *basileus*, distinguished archaeologically by his much bigger house, with its very large living/feasting hall. To later Greeks the title *basileus* signified a "king" or "monarch," and scholars, almost without exception, so translate it in the Homeric texts. Yet in the Homeric society the *basileus* had very little coercive power over his community and was, as well, subject to displacement by other ambitious men whose family wealth and personal abilities were on par with the chief's. These lesser local chiefs also bore the title of *basileus*.

The political power structure has been aptly described as a series of loosely ranked, competing pyramids, each made up of a *basileus*, his family, close kin, dependents and followers. In practice, a pyramid was often co-terminous with a village, although, especially in the larger villages, there might well be several such pyramids. The situation was complicated by the fact that a chief would also recruit followers outside his local base, that is, among the other *poleis* of the *demos*. Note that I have omitted mention of corporate kin groups as functional entities for social and political organization and integration, although they are prominent in ethnographic accounts of living tribal societies. Recent research has cast serious doubt on the existence of a gentilic system of interlocking clans, phratries and internal tribes, once universally believed to form the structure of early Greek communities.[2] In the absence of corporate clans and superclans the emphasis is put squarely on the individual household (the *oikos*) and its concentric circles of retainers and non-kin followers — exactly as we see in Homer.

Despite the looseness of the pyramid system, the Dark Age polity was not an uninhibited political free-for-all among competing groups as has been sometimes suggested. There was never a time in their entire history (including the radical democracies of the fifth and fourth centuries) that the Greeks did not recognize an apical figure who stood above and apart from all other leaders in the *demos* and who gave direction and set policy. In the pre-State period, this chief of chiefs, invariably the ranking chief of the main village, held only a tenuous dominance over the separate segments of the *demos*. He could claim no other title than the generic "*basileus*," and another claimant might easily take his place. Nevertheless, in the epics, the unifying office of paramount *basileus* is supremely important and necessary, and the legitimated holder is a figure of enormous respect and considerable authority.

Thus, Homer's Odysseus was the paramount chief of an ethnic group or tribe called the *Kephallenes* (conventionally anglicized to "Cephallenians"), who inhabited four islands and parts of the mainland opposite them. He was the chief of the main island of Ithaca, his home island, and lived in its main *polis*, also called Ithaca. When he went to Troy, he took with him a contingent of Cephallenian warriors, recruited not only from Ithaca village and island, but also from the other parts of his chiefdom. And back home, ninety-six of the 108 suitors and their followers, who hoped to usurp the office of paramount, came from the other islands, which were in effect autonomous political units.

Ethically, this was a warrior culture through and through, and the psychology and behaviours minutely detailed in both the *Iliad* and *Odyssey* parallel exactly those of the hundreds of small-scale warrior societies known to history and ethnography. A *basileus* was first and foremost a war-leader; there was no other route to elite status and no other way to stay at the top. The economy, like the politics, was bound up in the values of warriorship. This requires some elaboration. The Dark Age Greeks practised a mixed regime of subsistence farming and herding. The elite households shared this mode of life with the non-elite *oikoi*, but on a larger scale: bigger farm plots and work forces including slaves, and larger surpluses. The great distinction, however, between the rich and the average lay in numbers of animals. While most families owned some sheep and goats, a pair of oxen, and perhaps even some cattle (all pastured on common grazing grounds), the truly wealthy had numerous flocks and herds, especially of cattle, the most valued of the herd animals, and horses, the very emblem of a warrior nobility. Animals were considered to be the real wealth and can be said to represent a separate and more or less distinctively elite economic sphere. The other material measurement of prestige was "treasure" (*keimelia*, literally, "things laid up"), costly and scarce display items, principally fine cloth goods and metal objects (bronze, gold, silver, and iron), to which, again, the warrior elite had nearly exclusive access.[3]

Raiding, which ranged from sudden swoops to all-out sieges, and included armed extortion, was the fulcrum of the prestige economy, and was the basis for competition among chiefs. Ambitious warriors collected followers with inducements of profit and glory, sealing the bargain with lavish meat feasts. The object of raids was animals, booty and women, but especially animals. The chief's share, which included an extra leader's portion, replenished and — he would fervently hope — increased his flocks and herds, so that he could continue to give feasts, thereby outdoing his rivals and retaining the loyalty of his followers. The profit of this circular system of slaughtering animals to get animals, which somewhat precariously balanced income and outgo, was, of course, prestige and influence. Large flocks and store rooms full of display goods were proof of warrior excellence, and the mere sight of them ordained respect and subordination. The slaughter of those animals for feasts (including religious sacrificial feasts) was also the main redistributive function of a chief, and so a principal instrument of his social control.

Apart from the raid, the exchange (or "movement") of natural and man-made products occurred through gift-giving and trade. An intricate system, with codified rules about who gives to whom, when, and in what amount, served to validate relationships and regulate and calibrate status.[4] "Treasure" objects, particularly unused bronze tripods and cauldrons, were exchanged exclusively among the elite. These kinds of goods, never used as a purchasing medium, and circulating and re-circulating much like the Kula exchange of the Trobriand islanders, was the currency of prestige. As in most ranked societies, giving was a form of competition, and reputations were made and influence acquired by generous giving. On the other hand, stinginess was antithetical to leadership.

The pace of trade-exchange within the Greek world and with foreigners quickened after 900 B.C. By about 800, long-distance exchange had become regulated to the extent that Greek traders founded and maintained trade settlements in non-Greek lands. Imports were mainly confined to metal and luxury items from the Levant and Egypt — trophies of wealth and success. Only after 700, however, can we legitimately speak of a "trading sector" of the economy, and even then in a very modest sense compared to the later volume of trade.

From this brief description of the later Dark Age society, it is clear that Polanyi's three categories of economic integration — reciprocity, redistribution, and exchange — were totally submerged in institutions and values of a non-economic kind. Almost without exception, every economic (in the more purely materialist sense) gesture was reflexively a social gesture. The exception was a fledgling trading system, which, however, was essentially peripheral to the subsistence economy and quantitatively negligible until the seventh century. Here we should add — as Karl Polanyi pointed out long ago — that while Dark Age chiefs might engage in trade as a side activity of their piracy and mainly in pursuit of raw metals, they despised the occupation of trader on the grounds that it was not a warrior activity.[5]

We can give substance and life to these remarks by following Odysseus and his followers (*hetairoi* = "companions," "comrades") on their return from the Trojan War. This portion of the *Odyssey* is generally neglected as a reflection of the workings of the actual society. I think that is because these episodes contain the most fantastical elements in the epic, which makes them appear remote from real-life experience, and because the milieu is not a settled community, like Ithaca, Troy or Phaeacia, but a roving pirate-band. Yet, as was said above, the *hetairoi*-band is the basic political grouping, and the principal instrument of prestige and profit for its members, especially the chief. Moreover, we can assume a continuity in social relationship from raid to village life. Although things change somewhat when the warriors return home and are reintegrated into their own families, kindreds and villages, with the contrasting pulls of loyalty and energy these present, most *hetairoi* will nonetheless remain loyal to Odysseus and his house, and he to them. Nor is there any reason to think that the operation and motivation of reciprocity and redistribution will differ from peace to raid. What we see, then, in the adventures of Odysseus and his band of *hetairoi*, is the society in its purest, most distilled, form.

Odysseus himself, posing (in one of his many lying tales) as a once powerful Cretan warrior-chief, now a wandering exile, tells how one gathers a following, and why. Unable to settle down into dull domestic life after the Trojan War, and itching for adventure, he says,

> I outfitted nine ships, and the host gathered quickly. Then, for six days my trusty *hetairoi* feasted; and I supplied them with many victims, both for sacrifices to the gods and for them to make feasts for themselves; and on

the seventh day we embarked and sailed away from broad Crete... (*Od.* 14.248-51).

That is the way the "real" Odysseus and the other Greek chiefs would have recruited their companions for the Trojan War. The word for "feast," *dais*, is from the verb *daio*, "to distribute, divide." This etymology is one of the key semantic indicators of the highly reciprocal nature of the pre-state society.

The first leg of the return voyage is quite realistic — Homer eases his characters (and us, his audience) gradually into the realm of the fantastic — a raid against a Thracian tribe called the Cicones (9.39ff.). The raid began auspiciously; they swooped in from the sea, sacked the main village, killed the men, took away the women and "many possessions" (*ktemata polla*). According to the rule of raiding bands, "We divided it up (verb *daio*), so that no man would go deprived of his equal share" (42).

Immediately, however, troubles start; Odysseus gives the order to run (raids are essentially hit and run), but the men, like "foolish children" (*nepioi*), he says, stay on the beach and feast on the captured sheep, cattle and wine they had hoisted. The next morning reinforcements come from the inland villages of the Cicones. In a day-long battle by the ships they lose six men from each of the twelve ships before they get away.

Here I should say a word about numbers and realism. Twelve ships with (conventionally) fifty men each would be a force of 600 warrior-rowers. This is actually one of the smallest contingents in the Catalogue of Ships in the *Iliad* (Agamemnon, for example, leads 120 ships). Such numbers would have been impossible in the thinly populated Dark Age and highly improbable even for the archaic period. This poses no problem. We may conjecture that in real life Odysseus' entire Cephallenian chiefdom might have contained five or six thousand people (this would probably be a high estimate), with, say, a total of 800-1,000 men of fighting age. A major chief like

Odysseus might easily have been able to gather a troop (the Greek word is *laos*) of 100 or 150 men for a serious raid, i.e., not cattle-lifting and kidnapping, but a full-fledged attack against a prosperous village of 300-400 people, with, say, fifty to seventy-five fighting-age men. So, exaggeration of scale, an epic characteristic, poses no historical problem and does not affect the qualitative picture.

The Cicones episode introduces one of the recurring motifs of the adventures, the tension between the *basileus* and his often unruly *hetairoi*, who resist strict military discipline and regard themselves as equal among one another and nearly equal to their leader. This is the underlying contradiction of power relations in chiefdoms; followers will not always follow obediently. We observe this shifting of the quality and the extent of command authority not only here but throughout both epics. The *Odyssey* provides an especially revealing instance of the chief-people tension in Book 16 (418-48), which also gives us a glimpse into the relations between a paramount chief and a sub-chief. Penelope lectures Antinous, one of the main suitors, on his outrageous behaviour. She reminds him that his father, one of the Cephallenian chiefs, once had to flee the wrath of the local *demos* because he had joined up with the Taphian pirates in raiding against the Thesprotians, who at that time were allied to the Cephallenians. The people were angry enough to want to kill him and "eat up his great and pleasant livelihood." Though a chief, Antinous' father was quite vulnerable to the irritation of his people when they felt he had overstepped his authority. He managed to escape their punishment only by fleeing to Odysseus, who protected him until their anger cooled.

So, in this world of uncertain leadership, the extent and quality of control are highly circumstantial; sometimes the leader's authority is complete and unquestioned; at other times the people simply refuse to obey. There are no "constitutional" rules, only the leader's strength of body and character. Thus, in the next adventure, "The Lotus Eaters" (9.82-104), Odysseus is shown as exerting perfect control over his band. When a party of three men, sent to scout the situation, eat the lotus fruit and refuse to return, Odysseus himself goes and drags them out by force and ties them up in the ship and orders his fleet to sail on. Because it is a small mutiny and because the rest of the *hetairoi* agree with his actions, the desired harmony between chief and followers is preserved.

The episode of the Cyclops, which takes up the rest of Book 9 (105-566), begins with an appropriately "primitive" example of reciprocity. The deserted island opposite the land of the Cyclopes, where Odysseus had prudently landed them, was inhabited only by huge herds of wild goats. In this completely "feral" environment, totally removed from the familiar "tamed" world of villages, farms and pastures, Odysseus and his men reenact a social ritual as old as human society itself. Dividing into three hunting parties, they soon bring down much game. "Twelve ships followed me, and to each nine goats were allotted; but for me alone they chose out ten" (159-60). Afterwards, they feasted all day on goat-meat and drank the wine they had taken from the Cicones. The only thing that distinguishes this scene from an event in the life of a primitive, egalitarian hunting band — where the catch is divided evenly among everyone — is the "ten for me alone." This extra prize, the *geras*, or leader's special share, tells us we are looking at an established rank society, but in the primordial setting of the world of the pre-civilized Cyclopes — here Homer is a fine anthropologist — the reciprocity is pure. Odysseus does not keep the ten goats but shares them with his companions.[6] He receives his material due as leader, as a *symbolic* gift ratifying his position, which he immediately returns. His "profit" lies in having them to redistribute, building up his fund of good will; what he pockets is the honour, *time*.

On the next day Odysseus convenes an assembly to explain his plan to sail over to the land of the Cyclopes in his own ship, leaving the other eleven in the safety of the deserted island. At this point we should note that in this and all subsequent adventures, the action takes place within the more naturalistic confines of a single ship, and, indeed, with an even smaller number. For when they beached the ship, Odysseus chose "the twelve best of my *hetairoi*," to explore the cave of the Cyclops.

The *hetairoi* "beg" (*lissomai*) Odysseus to steal the cheeses and the sheep and goats, and quickly leave, but *ou pithomen*, "I did not listen to them," he says (228), hoping in his greed for treasure to see if he can extract some "guest-gifts" (*xeineia*) from the absent owner when he returns. As I have said, this kind of pull and tug forms the usual pattern of the leader-follower relationship. On the one hand, the leader displays those qualities that make him the leader — foresight, prudence, protectiveness — but also bad judgement and recklessness, that go against the common will and good. There should be no doubt in our minds that in portraying this tension and exploring this ambivalence from both perspectives — the rash disobedience of the *hetairoi*, the selfish stubbornness of the *basileus* — the poet is commenting on a *generic* problem.

In some respects Odysseus *is* the ideal chieftain, as in the planning and execution of the blinding of the Cyclops and escape from his cave. The Homeric *archos* ("leader") is ultimately the solitary figure on whom everything hinges. In his own words:

> But I was planning how things might turn out the very best, if I could find some way of escape for my *hetairoi* and for myself. And I wove in my mind all sorts of tricks and wiles (as one does in a matter of life and death), for a great evil was near us; and this seemed to my mind the best plan (420-24).

It should be emphasized that in every situation the leader is obligated to put his life on the line. In perfect symmetry with the apportionment of booty, danger is also apportioned in an egalitarian manner. For the perilous task of putting out the Cyclops' eye, four men are picked by casting lots, "and I was numbered fifth among them" (331-35). The leader is both inside and outside the allotment, of course; just as he always gets the extra *geras* he always gets the extra portion of the danger.[7]

Failure of leadership with its socially negative consequences is brought up again in the Polyphemus story. Once more, Odysseus courts disaster by going against the common will (and common sense) for his own personal glory. As they are escaping in their ship, against the entreaties of his companions he taunts the Cyclops, who almost swamps them with huge rocks. Worst of all, by boasting of his name and homeland he allows the giant to name him to his father, Poseidon, who fulfils his prayer to thwart the homecoming and "destroy utterly all his *hetairoi*" (473-542).

The episode of the Cyclops ends, as it had begun, with an example of equal sharing among the group. Odysseus and his surviving shipmates return to the other ships with the Cyclops' sheep. As they had done earlier in the goat hunt, "We divided [the sheep] so that no one would go cheated of his equal share; but my well-greaved *hetairoi* gave the ram to me alone, separate from the division of the sheep, and I sacrificed him on the shore to Zeus" (549-52). In an exact counterpart to the generalized reciprocity observed in egalitarian bands and tribes, all the *hetairoi* share in the spoils, including those who did not take part in the raid. The prize ram, Polyphemus' favourite animal, is fitting symbolic recognition of the leader's cunning and courage. His immediate return of the gift to the giving group completes the circle of reciprocity.

The social function of the rituals of sharing and feasting is to foster the spirit of unity and co-operation within the group. The *geras*, as we see in these examples of purely symbolic presentations, does not violate this spirit. At the same time, the leader's "due" (even if it is, as here, merely honorific and without resemblance to permanent gain), like his "right" to act as the distributor, sustains and strengthens the principle of centricity, of subordination to central authority, without which co-operative social order would be impossible.[8] Thus equal allotment and *geras*, which might appear to express contradictory principles, are a highly complementary means of balancing the conflicting claims of egalitarianism and authoritarianism which are inherent in the chiefdom.

Yet, despite the best efforts to avert it, that contradiction permanently lurks not far below the surface. In both the *Iliad* and the *Odyssey* this tension flares up so frequently that we cannot escape the conclusion that the epic tradition is exploring a recurrent, indeed nagging, social problem. Usually, as we saw in the Cyclops story, and will see again presently, the breakdown in reciprocity is triggered by the fact (or at least perception) that the leader is placing his own wealth and glory-needs before the common good. Just so, in the following episode (10.27-55), Aeolus, the divine keeper of the winds, has given Odysseus a bag containing the contrary winds, with the strict admonition not to open it. Thus protected, the ships sail within sight of Ithaca. Odysseus, weary from his long dutiful stint at the helm, falls asleep and his *hetairoi*, suspecting that Odysseus is holding out on them, grumble among themselves.

> Look, how dear and honoured this man is by the men to whose towns and lands he comes. He is bringing much fine treasure from the booty out of Troy, and we, who have completed the same journey, are returning home with empty hands. And now Aeolus, out of his friendship for him, has given him these gifts. But come, let us quickly see what these are, how much gold and silver are in the bag (10.38-45).

Once more, the built-in adversarial posture, which co-exists with the idealized leader-follower relationship, erupts to threaten the integrity of the group.

Their next adventure, in the land of the Laestrygonian cannibal giants, is a kind of doublet of the Cyclops episode and, for literary purposes, functions essentially as a plot device to lose the other eleven ships (10.76-132). Odysseus' ship, reduced now to a crew of forty-five, sails on, arriving finally at the island of Aeaea, home of the enchantress Circe, where Odysseus and his companions are, as always, the sole representatives of the human social order. This Eden-like environment becomes the setting for yet another mythic reenactment of primitive sharing and solidarity (133-574). Going off alone, to see if there was any sign of civilization, Odysseus comes across a giant stag, kills it, and with heroic effort carries it on his shoulders to his comrades lying on the beach, immobilized by despair, and revives their spirits with the "glorious feast." In this elemental act the twin senses of "divide" and "distribute" that lie behind *dais* are seamlessly combined. According to Elman Service, that is how ranked leadership began in the first place. Such generous service to one's fellows is a "starting mechanism" for the leadership role. By repeated acts of public benefit, an occasional leader comes to occupy a permanent position.[9] In this ultra-simplified setting the poet has Odysseus recreate the very origins of the political order.

Yet order is always poised for disorder in the Homeric world. For the first time, we are introduced to an actual opposing voice in the person of a man named Eurylochus, whom Odysseus describes as a "[close?] relative by marriage" (*peos*) (10.441), possibly his sister's husband, though we can only guess. Eurylochus, who comes off as rather a shirker and whiner, is also, we learn here, Odysseus' second in command. The geographical setting may be a fairy-tale primeval paradise, but the sociological milieu is the familiar one of a small village community.

We first see Eurylochus when, on the next morning (10.205), Odysseus divides his command in two, appointing himself leader of one group of twenty-two men and Eurylochus of the other. As usual, allotment is used to determine which of the two groups will have the dangerous job of exploring. After Eurylochus has lost his men to Circe's enchantments, Odysseus, ever the responsible leader, goes alone to Circe's house, forces her to turn his companions back into men, returns to the rest and announces the good news, that their comrades are alive and feasting in abundance. Eurylochus tries to dissuade them from going to Circe's, predictably blaming Odysseus' bad leadership for the loss of life in the Cyclops' cave: "For those men perished through this man's recklessness (*atasthalie*)" (431-37). This sort of situation, in which a lesser leader challenges the authority of the legitimate paramount, will have been a common occurrence in real life; every villager in the audience will have witnessed a similar scene many times.

Odysseus' immediate impulse — which reminds us again that personal might is literally an essential element of rule in this society — is to kill his challenger, but he is persuaded not to by the rest. We note that the confrontation doesn't end badly; Eurylochus goes along after all, in fear and shame. He doesn't even lose his rank, for twice more we see him in delegated positions of responsibility (11.23-24, 12.195-96).

In his final and fateful appearances as the self-appointed spokesman for the group, Eurylochus again shows how easily a chief's authority is subverted by a forceful opposing voice from below, especially when it purports to speak for the common good. Having escaped, though with losses, from the hideous trials of Charybdis and Scylla (12.234-59), there awaits the last test of the forbidden Cattle of the Sun. Even though their survival thus far was due to Odysseus' good leadership ("my courage, planning and intelligence," is how he puts it, 12.211), the men are exhausted and totally demoralized. So, when Odysseus wisely orders them not to land on the island of the Sun, but row past, "the spirit was broken within them, and immediately Eurylochus answered me with hateful words," giving an impassioned and persuasive speech to the effect that in a night sail they would all perish. "And the rest of the companions gave assent" (*eneon alloi hetairoi*), a standard formula for agreement to an opinion voiced in assembly.

Odysseus reluctantly gives in: "you [pl.] force [*biazete*] me, one man alone" (297), but still has sufficient authority to make them swear an oath not to eat the Cattle of the Sun. When they are becalmed on the island for a month, and starving, Eurylochus delivers another persuasive speech for slaughtering the cattle, which ends: "'I would rather lose my life once and for all gulping at a wave than to pine slowly away on a deserted island.' So spoke Eurylochus, and the rest of the companions gave assent" (12.340-52).

I doubt there exists a clearer description in all of ethnography of a low-level chiefdom, and of its internal stresses, than in these books of the *Odyssey*. The chief possesses considerable authority and power, but he must bend to the collective will of the fighting men, who are naturally disposed to be critical of his leadership. It is important that we understand that the epic tradition constantly underscores the fact that the leader-people tension is the cause of social dysfunction. Odysseus is consistently represented as being as good a leader as a people could realistically hope for; yet the message is unmistakable, that personal leadership is fragile and unstable and that the intrinsic opposition between the two social vectors of autocracy on the one hand and egalitarianism on the other, is a frequent prescription for social breakdown.

We may add an Odyssean postscript that highlights this problem. None of the *hetairoi* made it back to Ithaca. Had Odysseus returned with his follower-band intact, the constitutional crisis that had been brewing at home would have dissolved immediately. As it was, Telemachus, a boy just becoming a man, was in a very precarious position, with no brothers, cousins or kinsmen by marriage to help him stave off the suitors, but only a handful of *hetairoi* loyal to the house, too few and too old to be of much use, and a populace that naturally blamed Odysseus for the loss of their sons, husbands and brothers.[10] And so, when Odysseus returned alone he had to lay low and scheme. By his fabled cunning and by recruiting a rag-tag band of followers from his loyal slaves he saved his chieftainship and the preeminence of the house of Laertes. Still, it took the intervention of the gods to prevent a civil war and restore the established order.[11]

In the event, the low-level chiefdom form of polity, which, despite its inherent instability, was quite serviceable in the simple conditions of the Dark Age, was doomed to vanish in the face of a whole new set of conditions, often referred to as a "social revolution." As the population rose sharply in the eighth century and land became a scarce good, the prestige economy, based on large herds and raids for animals and booty, rapidly gave way to an agricultural economy based on exclusive landownership, surplus cereal and oil production, and wage labour. Those changes not only ended the social organization by follower-bands, they also saw the replacement of the traditional morality of reciprocity and sharing, of the sort we have observed in the story of Odysseus, by a value of exploitation.[12]

How the historically unique polity of the mature city-state evolved out of the thick stew of change, growth and conflict, is a matter of lively discussion and controversy. Historians of this process, which unfolds during the archaic period (roughly 700-490) and well into the classical period (roughly 490-350), would do well to order the kaleidoscope of events and transitions on the three Polanyian categories of reciprocity (whose imperative was a major social-psychological force in this period), redistribution (which took on some very interesting forms in the developing city-state) and market exchange (whose evolutionary effect became strong, if not decisive, late in the fifth century). When we look at archaic and classical history in this way, the break between the pre-historical Dark Age and the historical era seems much less severe than how it is represented in the history books. The citizen-soldier of the democratic city-state is imprinted with the egalitarian ethic of Odysseus' *hetairoi*-band.

## Notes

1. The following sketch of the Dark Age society is my own interpretation of the evidence, for which see Donlan 1982; 1985; 1989. On the controversial question of the relation of epic poetry to the actual society, see Raaflaub 1991; Morris 1986 (both with ample bibliography).
2. Roussel 1976; Bourriot 1976.
3. On the various "spheres" of the "multi-centric" Homeric economy, marked by different institutionalization and different moral values (which have numerous anthropological parallels), see Donlan 1981. This concept goes back to Polanyi's distinction between "general-purpose" and "special-purpose" money.
4. On gift-giving in Homeric society see M. I. Finley's *World of Odysseus* (Finley 1978). This short book, first published in 1954, introduced the ideas of Polanyi and the "substantivist" school of economic history into the study of Homeric society and began a new chapter in the historiography of early Greece.
5. Polanyi 1951, 25–26.
6. On equal shares and the leader's extra due, see *Od.* 14.229-34; *Il.* 11.677–705.
7. See Finley 1978, 96–97.
8. Sahlins 1972, 189-90.
9. Service 1965, 149; Sahlins 1972, 208.
10. As Eurylochus had done, Eupeithes, the father of the suitor Alcinous, takes control of the people by whipping up sentiment against Odysseus in the assembly for losing "many good men and the hollow ships" in the return (24.426–88; cf. 462–66).
11. 24.472–86: Zeus decrees that the Ithacans should swear an oath for Odysseus "to be *basileus* forever" and that they should all "love one another as before, and let wealth and peace abound." Cf. 546–48.
12. Already by the turn of the eighth to the seventh century, Hesiod in *Works and Days* is complaining about the greed of the *basileis* and their disregard for "justice" *(dike)*, the abstract quality of balanced reciprocity.

## References

Bourriot, Felix. 1976. *Recherches sur la nature du génos: étude d'histoire sociale athénienne. Périodes archaïque et classique.* Paris: H. Champion.
Donlan, Walter. 1981. "Scale, Value, and Function in the Homeric Economy." *American Journal of Ancient History* 6:101–17.
———. 1982. "Reciprocities in Homer." *Classical World* 75:137–75.
———. 1985. "The Social Groups of Dark Age Greece." *Classical Philology* 80:293–308.
———. 1989. "The Pre-State Community in Greece." *Symbolae Osloenses* 64:5–29.
Finley, Moses I. 1978. *The World of Odysseus*. 2d rev. ed. New York: Viking.
Morris, Ian. 1986. "The Use and Abuse of Homer." *Classical Antiquity* 5:81–138.

Polanyi, Karl. 1951. "Reciprocity and Redistribution in Homeric Greece." Chapter One of the *Greek Manuscript*, on which see Tandy and Neale in this volume.
Raaflaub, Kurt. 1991. "Homer und die Geschichte des 8. Jh. v. Chr." In *Zweihundert Jahre Homer-Forschung: Ruckblick und Ausblick*, edited by Joachim Latacz, 205–55. Stuttgart and Leipzig: B. G. Teubner.
Roussel, Denis. 1976. *Tribu et cité: études sur les groupes sociaux dans les cités grecques aux époques archaïque et classique*. Paris: Les Belles Lettres.
Sahlins, Marshall D. 1972. *Stone Age Economics*. Chicago: Aldine.
Service, Elman. 1965. *Primitive Social Organization: An Evolutionary Perspective*. New York: Random House.

# 3

## The Community Against the Market in Classical Athens*

**Ian Morris**

Ancient Greece was central to Karl Polanyi's case for substantivism. *The Great Transformation* remains Polanyi's most influential work, but within months of its appearance he had decided that to explain the uniqueness of the disembedding of western European economies in the nineteenth century, he needed to adopt a much broader historical framework. On joining the faculty at Columbia University in 1947, he began a series of seminars which culminated in the publication of *Trade and Market in the Early Empires*, ten years later.[1] At that time, ancient economic history was strongly formalist, emphasizing economic growth and the rise of an entrepreneurial middle class as the driving forces in the seventh and sixth centuries, followed by an economic crisis, inflation, and decline in the late fifth and fourth.[2] If this interpretation was correct, then Polanyi's general thesis of the extreme peculiarity of modern economic arrangements would be substantially weakened; so, not surprisingly, he turned his attention to Greece.

Polanyi's unpublished lectures on Greek economic history were collected after his death as *The Livelihood of Man*, but in *Trade and Market* he included a major paper on two of the central texts in the modernizing interpretation of Greek economics: Aristotle's discus-

---

* This paper was originally delivered at the fourth International Polanyi Conference, held in Montréal in November 1992. I would like to thank the editors of this volume and Walter Neale for inviting me to take part, and the University of Chicago for financial support.

sions of exchange in the *Ethics* (1132b31-33b28) and *Politics* (1256b26-57b39).³ Polanyi started from a conundrum among contemporary scholars of antiquity, who took for granted the assumptions of neoclassical economics: if Aristotle was a timeless genius, why were his ventures into economic thought so incompetent and pedestrian? For the fact was that the Stagirite seemed strangely unable to comprehend the workings of the self-regulating market system.

This was Polanyi's starting point for questioning the existence of a market economy in classical Athens. He argued that, in fact, Aristotle was being particularly clever in these passages, working out for the very first time a theory of equivalence. The difficulties of these texts were to be explained by the fact that as Aristotle was writing, in the 330s B.C., an independent market was for the first time emerging out of the wider social framework. Even in the fifth century, the era of Pericles and the Parthenon, the economy had been embedded in society.

Polanyi's article revolutionized the study of the Greek economy.⁴ Some historians continue to resist its implications,⁵ but others have developed it in new directions. The most important among these was Moses Finley, who was completing his Ph.D. at Columbia University during Polanyi's first five years there. Finley held a position at Rutgers during this period, but frequently attended Polanyi's seminar. Polanyi's methodological influence is clearly visible in Finley's *Studies in Land and Credit in Ancient Athens* and *The World of Odysseus*; but Finley distanced himself from Polanyi on empirical matters. He declined to contribute to *Trade and Market*, and a few years after Polanyi's death published his own interpretation of Aristotle.⁶ Finley argued that Polanyi had been insensitive to the context of the passages he was discussing, and had ignored the fact that Aristotle examined exchange as part of a larger consideration of the ethical dimensions of the Greek city-state (the *polis*). Finley suggested that "nowhere in the *Politics* does Aristotle ever consider the rules or mechanisms of commercial exchange. On the contrary, his insistence on the unnaturalness of commercial gain rules out the possibility of such a discussion.... Of economic analysis there is not a trace."[7] Finley went further than Polanyi: for him, Aristotle did not discover the economy, because even in the late fourth century it was not there. There was no "disembedding," and Aristotle was interested only in identifying the ethical basis for exchange in a community of equal citizens.

Like Polanyi, Finley explicated Aristotle in order to justify a larger argument. In *The Ancient Economy*, he suggested that at no time in Greek or Roman antiquity was there anything resembling an autonomous market system or serious economic thought, and that a single model of an embedded economy was applicable to the whole period from about 700 B.C. to A.D. 500. Finley never explicitly denied that there was economic growth in antiquity, but that is certainly the implication of *The Ancient Economy*. His famous paper on technological innovation in antiquity — or rather, the lack of it — also implies that the prevalence of slave labour ruled out any major economic growth.[8] Greek historians often adopt a "synchronic" approach as a response to the paucity of sources for social and economic issues, treating the whole period from 430 to 322 as a single phase;[9] and not surprisingly, those sympathetic to substantivism have had little reason to question Finley's position. However, some Romanists, even those favourable to Finley, have generally concluded that the empire did experience economic growth on a large scale; the increase in the city of Rome's population to more than a million in the first century B.C. drew large parts of the Mediterranean world into a market relationship with it.[10] The evidence is less clear in the case of Athens, but in this paper I try to combine Finley's emphasis on the centrality of the community with Polanyi's insight that economic growth *did* take place in Greek history.

Briefly, I argue that the Athenian *polis* was based on the idea that 1) exchange for gain automatically created inequalities, and that all such inequalities should be pushed as far as possible outside the community, where they could not threaten the ideal equality of the citizens. Consequently, 2) the community as a whole tried to relegate market operations to marginal groups, and especially excluded foreigners or slaves. The problem was that 3) during the fifth century the scale of military operations escalated dramatically, causing the city-states to need much larger sums of money than previously. This created new demands on the rich which were difficult to cope with within the traditional framework of a community of equals; and 4) by 400 B.C. the social structure of the *poleis* had shifted to allow much more room for wealthy elites to express themselves as such. Whether 3) caused 4), or whether they were interrelated in more complex ways, is a complicated issue which needs to be tackled at greater length than this paper allows.[11] Here, I argue that Polanyi was right to link Aristotle's discussion of exchange to contemporary developments, but I see these as being social as much as economic. Aristotle was waging a rear-guard action, defending the idea of the *polis* as a community of equals at a time when other, larger and more hierarchical, social systems were becoming politically dominant in the eastern Mediterranean.

## Citizens of Athens

Aristotle's *Politics*, written in the 330s, is our best guide to Greek social structure. It was based on studies of 158 states produced by Aristotle's students. These are largely lost, and the relationship of our text to them is obscure. Comparisons with other sources suggest that the *Politics* is highly empirical, although Aristotle did try to force the data into his own elitist philosophical agenda. In our second major source, his *Ethics*, he argued that inquiry should always begin from popular beliefs about phenomena (1095a 28, 1142b2-8).[12]

The Athenians accepted that there were differences between citizens, and in some regards a definite aristocracy can be said to have existed. Some within the *polis* could claim to be "well born" (defined by Aristotle at *Politics* 1301b1-4; *Rhetoric* 1360b31-38, 1367b28-32). Their background gave them certain advantages (*Politics* 1291b 29-30), but in no sense did they constitute an aristocratic order like that of most pre-industrial societies.[13] The reasons for the relative weakness of classical aristocrats lie in the complex events of the eighth to sixth centuries, but by the fifth century the Athenian community as a whole claimed the right to use the law, exercised through popular lawcourts, to minimize elite privileges (e.g., Plato, *Apology* 24D-25C; Demosthenes 21.45). Rich citizens who flaunted their wealth and refused to follow proper norms of behaviour could be brought down through prosecutions (e.g., Lysias 14; 20.19; Demosthenes 21.133, 158). The infamous sycophants, decried by elite writers as parasites who brought self-serving cases against quiet rich men, can actually be seen as structurally crucial to democracy.[14]

The Athenians saw their *polis* as a community of "middling citizens," or *metrioi*, characterized by "like-mindedness" (*homonoia*). The *metrios* was content with "a little" money, and could be contrasted with both the rich and the poor. But wealth was not the only consideration, and even a rich liturgist could be called *metrios* if he lived properly. He was defined through everyday actions — doing good for his family and for the community, having a strong sense of shame, and above all, having his appetites under control.[15]

Citizens saw themselves as a group of *metrioi*, tied together by *philia*, perhaps best translated as "balanced reciprocity."[16] They idealized the *polis* as a community under threat from marginal groups which lacked the virtues of the *metrioi*. A man judged to stand at any extreme was one who lacked control. In Winkler's words, he was

> socially deviant in his entire being, whose deviance was principally observable in behaviour that flagrantly violated or contravened the dominant social definition of masculinity ... the *kinaidos*, mentioned only with laughter

or indignation, is the unreal, but dreaded, antitype behind every man's back.[17]

The rich man, especially if young, was seen as prone to *hybris*, "the serious assault on the honour of another, which is likely to cause shame, and lead to anger and attempts at revenge."[18] Aristotle (*Rhetoric* 1378b28-29) explains that "they think that in this they show their superiority," and after an exhaustive study, Fisher concludes that *hybris* was "constantly seen as a major crime, endangering the cohesion of the community as well as the essential self-esteem and identity of the individual."[19]

Poverty, on the other hand, forced a man to do undignified things, making him vulnerable to exploitation. Halperin suggests that in popular thought the poor,

> deprived of their autonomy, assertiveness, and freedom of action — of their masculine dignity, in short — were in danger of being assimilated not only to slaves but to prostitutes, and so ultimately to women: they were at risk of being effeminized by poverty.

The true *metrios* ought to be a self-sufficient farmer on his own land, head of a household, married with children, responsible, and self-controlled. The phalanx provided a useful metaphor for the solidarity and interdependence of the citizens.[20]

We know little about the distribution of wealth, and whether there really was a substantial "middle class" in economic terms. But what is certain is that many of the citizens listening to court speeches must have been poor or even landless, and less than one-third were hoplites. But by general agreement — a willing suspension of disbelief — they thought of each other as *metrioi* and *philoi*: "rich" and "poor" became categories of exclusion. Whatever its economic basis, the philosophy of the *metrios* was a useful democratic fiction, a powerful structuring principle that guided behaviour. A full share in the community, and therefore in its politics, flowed directly from the fact of being born a free male: as Halperin bluntly puts it, "the symbolic language of democracy proclaimed on behalf of each citizen, 'I, too, have a phallus'."[21]

The exclusion of women and the near impossibility of naturalization were not unfortunate quirks in an otherwise admirable system. The strong principle of equality was essentialist. Everyone who was born an Athenian man was a *metrios*, deserving equal respect and an equal share in the social goods of the community, unless he forfeited them. It is a mistake to see a contradiction between egalitarianism and exclusionary practices; the Athenians simply assumed a different space for equality from liberal thinkers. It is equally mistaken to avoid the issue of exclusion by arguing that women's membership in the geographical community made up for their absence from the political community. What mattered was that Athens was a group of *metrioi*. Every *metrios* had a share in the community, and no one else had any share at all. To widen citizenship to include women or freed slaves would mean scrapping the entire social order.[22]

The *metrioi* were supposed to be a community of *philoi* — not "friends," as it is usually poorly translated, but equal, interdependent citizens (Aristotle, *Ethics* 1171b32).[23] Plato (*Laws* 757A) and Aristotle (*Ethics* 1157b35) both equated the abstract noun *philia* with equality (*isotes*). Aristotle argued that inequality would destroy *philia* (*Ethics* 1158b11-59a5). One form of inequality, he argued, was produced through market exchange, where one man exploited another. The man who aims primarily at making money is defined by Aristotle (*Ethics* 1096a5-6) as "someone who lives under restraint" (i.e., he subordinates himself to the pursuit of wealth, which should be a means, not an end). Aristotle goes on to argue that any man living for the sake of another, under any kind of restraint, cannot be truly free, and hence cannot be a true citizen (*Rhetoric* 1367a32). To stay for a moment with Aristotle's philosophizing, in his ideal state, wealth production would be merely the means to sustain the meaningful associations of the household and the *polis* (*Politics* 1256b30-34), and would be carried out by non-citizens (1278a6-8, 1329a2-39). Aristotle's basic premise is that the best things have attained a form which is natural (*Politics* 1252b30-53a1). Slavery must therefore be natural; and in an infamous passage he argues against other contemporary thinkers that this is indeed the case (*Politics* 1253b23-55b40).[24]

Economic relationships within the *polis* were to be reciprocal ones of lending and borrowing. Their typical form was the *eranos* loan, where a citizen who needed money would ask *philoi* — either kin or "friends" — for help. The *philoi* would then try to scrape up the money, which would be lent without interest. The borrower was obliged to repay it, and might have to put up some assurance, and anyone who failed to repay committed a gross offence against the *philia*, and might be dragged through the lawcourts. Only those marginalized from *polis* society would have regular recourse to professional lenders, themselves often aliens or slaves.[25]

**Other Residents of Athens**

Of course, Aristotle's representation can be criticized for its blatant elitism and its teleological systematization; but on the whole, his account of the ideology of Athens does seem to fit with the practices which we see in many other texts.[26] Loraux points out that this kind of agreement arises partly because the Greeks wanted to think of their communities as harmonious and moral wholes, free from conflict,[27] but the fact that internal strife was more common than they suggest does not minimize the sociological significance of this idealized social structure.[28] Aristotle himself acknowledges very strongly the divisions within *poleis*, particularly those between rich and poor,[29] but it seems that the Athenians *did* try to relegate economic exploitation to non-citizen groups.

This statement raises complex source problems, because the ancient evidence does not allow us to quantify the involvement of citizens and non-citizens in industrial activity and retail or other forms of trade. The sources are mainly legal speeches, in which the speaker often has reason to be vague about the exact status of the people involved in the suit.[30] But ever since Hasebroek's *Trade and Politics*,[31] it has been clear that a substantial number of non-Athenians were heavily involved in Athenian maritime trade. Much of the import trade was in grain, which was vital to the Athenians if they were to survive, but they never attempted to put it under purely Athenian control. Even anti-Hasebroek historians have to concede that non-Athenians played a major part in financing Athenian trade.[32]

It is not necessary to argue that all, or even most, trade was in non-Athenian hands; just that non-citizens were heavily over-represented, which indicates a serious effort to alienate commercial exchanges beyond the citizen community, where they could not taint the *philia* of true *metrioi*. This is not a "primitivist" position, playing down the importance or volume of trade and industry. The best way to understand the Athenian situation is through the model of "transactional orders" developed by Bloch and Parry. In many cultures, perhaps all, market exchange is frequently presented as the location of immoral exploitation, and as a corrosive force threatening the ideal order. Disembedded commerce gives free rein to greed, which then disrupts "proper" relationships of piety, deference, kinship, etc. But as Bloch and Parry observe, "all these systems make — indeed *have* to make — some ideological space within which individual acquisition is a legitimate and even laudable goal; but ... such activities are consigned to a separate sphere which is ideologically articulated with, and subordinate to, a sphere of activity concerned with the cycle of long-term reproduction."[33] This is as true of the "disembedded" culture of 1990s America[34] as it was of ancient Greece. From the very earliest times, inter-annual variability in rainfall will have meant that long-distance trade in foodstuffs was common, and this can have been handled through disembedded exchanges as well as through gifts.³⁵ Regardless of the scale of marketing, Greek writers from the seventh century onward saw it as something opposed to a golden age when children respected parents, neighbours honoured neighbours, and all revered the gods. In Hesiod's *Works and Days* Perses' greed must be brought back in line with the divine and human balance, and three hundred years later in Isaeus' inheritance suits, grasping relatives still threaten familial respect (e.g., 5.30; 9.25). The Athenians' solution to the perennial problem of balancing the two transactional orders was to try to relegate the market to non-citizens.

The most obvious such group was the metics, or resident aliens, who lived in significant numbers in most *poleis*. These communities were frequently heavily involved in inter-community trade.³⁶ So far as we know, virtually all classical *poleis* restricted landholding to citizens, so anyone losing his own citizenship would be forced to turn to some kind of commercial activity. More importantly, given the strength of feeling against market relationships between citizens, the easiest way for a citizen of one *polis* to operate as a trader would be to settle temporarily or permanently in another. He would temporarily accept various legal disabilities in order to win wealth, which could later be transferred to his home *polis*, making him a respectable pillar of the community without any of the taint that came from exploiting his fellow citizens through the market.³⁷

Burke has argued that the appearance in 355 B.C. of Xenophon's strange tract called the *Ways and Means*, offering various ways for Athens to raise money, was a symptom of the disembedding of the Athenian economy.³⁸ I am less convinced of this. I would suggest that the financial crisis brought on by defeat in the Social War merely provided the motivation for Xenophon to publish a collection of time-honoured ideas about how to push exploitative economic activities out of the citizen community, onto metics. Burke points out that over the next thirty years, Athenian leaders did adopt several of the ideas suggested by Xenophon, as well as instituting various new schemes such as subsidized housing and faster legal processes for foreigners; but that does not mean either that they got these ideas from the *Ways and Means* or that these ideas represented a radically new attitude to trade and foreigners in the later fourth century. One of Xenophon's main arguments was that Athens should encourage metics to come to the city, since they brought in large revenues (2.1-3.13). Throughout, he seems to assume that merchants (*emporoi*) and shipowners (*naukleroi*) will be non-Athenians. When he argues that another major source of revenue for Athens would be a state fleet of merchant ships, he suggests that Athens could then "lease them under securities" (3.14: *ekmisthoun ep' engueton*). He does not explicitly say "lease them to metics," but doing so would produce more wealth for Athens as a whole than leasing them to citizens, and I think it is reasonable to argue that Xenophon assumed that the majority of traders would be non-Athenians; and that the majority of non-Athenians in Athens would be traders.

The role of slaves in economic production is even more controversial. Finley argued convincingly that the Athenians began importing large numbers of deracinated chattel slaves, mainly non-Greek, in the sixth century, following Solon's reforms of 594.[39] Solon effectively ended serfdom at Athens. The seventh-century elite had relied on serf labour to work their fields; unable to coerce Athenians to provide this any more, they turned to the only alternative — slaves. Finley was clear that the most important role for slaves was in agriculture, although he never committed himself to an opinion on how far down the social ladder slavery went. For his argument, it was enough to establish that the rich used slaves in their fields and that this was a crucial part of the survival of a free citizenry. As he argued, "one aspect of Greek history, in short, is the advance, hand in hand, of slavery *and* freedom."[40]

The actual evidence for slaves in the fields is poor; they are documented as having served mainly in the silver mines and in various industrial occupations.[41] Jameson argued that given the small size of most Athenian farms — probably just three to six hectares — the only way for most Athenians to support a family would be by very intensive agriculture; and that in such a system slave field-hands would more than earn their own keep.[42] However, Wood has denied this.[43] After a philological analysis of Xenophon's *Estate Manager* she suggests that most of the words usually translated as "slave" could equally well refer to free labourers, and that agricultural slavery was in fact virtually non-existent. Instead, the rich leased out land to poorer farmers, or else hired them to work their fields. In this way, the economic system functions without slavery: the rich get a profit from their estates, and the poor farmers augment the meagre produce of their own fields by renting others or drawing a wage. Robin Osborne has independently argued on demographic grounds that far more estates were leased out in Athens than most historians realize.[44]

Wood believes that elitist biases in the late eighteenth century led historians of Greece to assume that the Athenian poor must be a feckless, idle mob relying on slave labour; and that the debate initiated by Mitford set a pattern which no one has broken.[45] Wood's book is full of brilliant insights, but I believe that she is ultimately mistaken in this argument. Finley has shown that the historiography of slavery is much more complex than this, and Jameson successfully undermines her philological analysis. Further, recent archaeological work suggests strongly that the kind of highly intensive agriculture hypothesized by Jameson did in fact characterize much of Greece from the late sixth to the second century B.C.[46] Wood may be right that renting land played a larger role in the economy than the Finleyan school has accepted, but the basic point that the normative exploitative relationship in Athenian agriculture was between citizens and junior members of their families or between citizens and non-citizen slaves, rather than between rich and poor citizens, remains unshaken. Athenian slaves were deeply divided by their varied origins and residential distribution among separate households, and never coalesced as a class group in opposition to the slave-owners.[47]

A third non-citizen group onto which labour was pushed was women. Women, although necessary for the biological reproduction of the *polis*, were not citizens. Like metics and slaves, they were too fragmented to form a class group in an antagonistic relationship to the male citizens.[48] However, it does not mean that Athenian women found no ways to resist exploitation, nor that they had no forms of association of their own.[49] Direct evidence for women's labour is minimal; the fullest account is Xenophon's strange story of Socrates' conversation with Ischomachus about the latter's wife (*Estate Manager* 7.3-10.13). What is clear is that men appropriated women's productive and reproductive labour. For Aristotle, this exploitation was perfectly in accordance with a *polis* of equal citizens because, by nature, women (like slaves, although he insisted that women were not the same as slaves: *Politics* 1252b1-8) were inferior to men, and meant to be ruled over (*Politics* 1254b13-15, 1259a39-b2, 1260a9-14). It was therefore perfectly acceptable for them to be involved in inherently exploitative relationships.

### Citizens and Public Finance

So far I have been talking about "classical Greece" as a static entity, based on sources dating from the 380s to the 330s B.C. Yet a dynamic element is vital if we are to understand the way the community opposed the market.

The nature of sixth-century trade is controversial,[50] but it is clear that economic relationships of all kinds were on a much smaller scale than those of the fifth century. Without reverting to the *Hauswirtschaft* model of Bücher, I believe that it is reasonable to see a great deal of self-sufficiency within the archaic *poleis*. There is no reason to see the grain trade as a very large-scale or permanent phenomenon before the early fifth century.[51] Similarly, state financial operations were rudimentary. Wars were fought almost entirely by citizen levies, and naval warfare was very small-scale. The big change came with the Persian wars of 490-479, which forced the Greeks to form a large military alliance under Spartan control. After a brief diplomatic tussle in 479/8, this passed under the control of the Athenians, who proceeded to exact tribute from their "allies" to pay for a fleet.[52] The tribute was probably generally paid by the rich in the subject states, and most of it went as pay for rowers in the fleet, causing it to be redistributed to the poor, both in Athens and the subject states.[53] But perhaps more importantly, wealth was redistributed from the Aegean as a whole toward Athens. Through this process of state-building,[54] Athens assumed control of vital economic resources such as minerals and large amounts of land, and increasingly tried to regulate political behaviour in the empire. By the 440s, Athens had a large financial reserve of 9,700 talents (Thucydides 2.13); but the cost of waging war with huge fleets and armies had escalated so much that by the early 420s Athens had probably run through most of its money.[55]

Thucydides tells us that in 427, "The Athenians ... for the first time raised from their own citizens a contribution (*eisphora*) of 200 talents" (3.19). There is considerable argument over whether he means the first time ever, the first time during the Peloponnesian War (i.e., since 431), or the first time that they had raised such a large sum,[56] but in the years that followed, the Athenians demanded more and more money from their rich citizens. At the same time, new styles of warfare were forcing the Athenians to allow a more professionalized military elite to emerge.[57] Nor were these changes unique to Athens: in order to win the war, the Spartans were forced to raise a fleet and to revolutionize their own military and financial operations.[58] In the process, their traditional political structures were almost completely destroyed by the power amassed by Lysander in 405-403 (Diodorus Siculus 14.13; Plutarch, *Lysander* 24-26),[59] and their social structure came close to the same fate in Cinadon's failed revolt, probably in 399 (Xenophon, *Hellenika* 3.3.4-11).

The Athenian rich were seeking ways to avoid the new burdens of taxation before 400 B.C., and in the fourth century, after the loss of the empire, they increasingly managed to do so. It is unclear whether these financial problems and the associated class tensions were the result of the rich being less willing to pull their weight, or the poor making excessive demands.[60] But the result is not in doubt: the Athenian financial structure increased in complexity. Even quite early in the fourth century, there were important changes, such as the allocation of money directly to officials like architects, without any control by the Assembly, and by 350, something of a financial elite was taking shape under men like Eubulus and Lycurgus.[61] Beginning in the 380s there was a divorce between political leaders and generals, and by the third quarter of the century mercenary soldiers were replacing citizen levies. This was a logical step in the military environment of the 340s and 330s, but it further eroded the ideal of citizen equality and interchangeability.[62] By the time of Demosthenes' Areopagus Decree in 343, even the principles of democratic rule seem to have been open to question. In order to preserve their dominance over Greece after 404, the Spartans might have needed to develop in similar ways; but their king Agesilaos bitterly resisted this, and Spartan power collapsed in 371.

### Changes in Citizen Behaviour

Associated with the new complexity in financial affairs and the new role of the rich beginning around 425 is a wave of evidence for a new self-confidence on the part of the wealthy. Throughout the first three-quarters of the fifth century, the rich had avoided any kind of material displays of their wealth; virtually no rich burials or lavish private houses are known from anywhere in Greece. Personal dress and display were muted; but communal projects, such as state sacrifices, or building temples or fortifications, were carried out on a massive scale. Beginning around 425, there was a major shift in material practices. Suddenly huge private tombs appear everywhere, and from 400 onward rich houses, with double courtyards, peristyles, and mosaic floors, appear at Athens, Eretria, Olynthus, and several other sites. There was a decline in temple building, and at Athens at least, a series of attempts to cut back on public, state-sponsored sacrifices in favour of a more personalized style of religion; and new, more flamboyant styles of elite dress emerged in the late fifth century.[63]

The archaeological evidence is difficult to interpret, but it seems to provide clear evidence for a major shift in attitudes in the late fifth century. The kind of reciprocal ideal described by Aristotle would perhaps have been a little closer to actual practices in the fifth century than in the fourth. I do not believe that the material record indicates a "fourth-century crisis" and collapse of the city-state ideology,[64] but it does indicate a certain loosening of the radically egalitarian ethos of the fifth century. The community of equals was breaking up under the pressure of economic growth fuelled by military competition. By the 330s, the likely date of Aristotle's *Politics*, that process had still not gone very far. Ober points out that the financial wizards of late fourth-century Athens only constituted a political elite in a very limited sense, and most of our evidence for deliberate exclusion of market principles in fact only dates to the 330s and 320s. As Finley showed, Aristotle was not grappling with the first signs of a market economy; and there was no disembedding of the economy in the late fourth, third, or any subsequent century B.C.[65]

Following Ober,[66] I would suggest that Aristotle's obsessive interest in the ethical basis of the citizen community was a response to the pressures he could see operating against that community not just in terms of the growth in scale which I have described above, but also through the threat to the city-states from the vastly larger power of Macedon. Aristotle had served as tutor to Alexander, later to be the conqueror of Persia, and son of the Philip who subdued Greece in 338. He could hardly have been unaware of the eclipse of the *polis* as a military power, but the *Politics* gives no hint of this. Strauss argues that Aristotle was sympathetic to Macedon, and that this partly explains his hostility to Athenian democracy;[67] but the situation may be more complicated. Aristotle's ideal state has little or nothing in common with Macedon, and there is little in Aristotle's surviving letters to Philip, Alexander, and Antipater to suggest that, like Plato, he hoped to use a powerful ruler to set up his ideal state. Other than the fact that he relied on Alexander's protection during his residence in Athens from 335 to 323,[68] it is hard to see why he would have been a Macedonian sympathizer. We should adopt the same perspective as did Polanyi in his response to conventional discussions of Aristotle's "economics": it seems more sensible to assume that the philosopher had a reason for doing what he did rather than claiming he was incapable of understanding his world. His reason was perhaps a desperate attempt to justify a vanishing social order.

There seems to be a close fit between the economic growth of the *polis* and the disintegration of the ideas of equality which demanded that market exchange should be alienated beyond the citizen community. I suggest that what we see after 350 is not the partial disembedding of the market identified by Burke, but a redefinition of "equality," so that it gradually became more legitimate for citizens to engage in economic transactions in which one party profited from the other. Runciman argues that the social relations of the *polis* were an evolutionary dead end, which had to be destroyed if more efficient social organisms were to appear.[69] Yet the destruction of the *polis* with its ideal of *philia* was also the destruction of ancient democracy.[70]

### Conclusion

The story of the *polis* poses some serious issues. Is social equality possible in a market system? Is a complex but non-market economy a possibility outside a small-scale agrarian city-state? Does the alienation of exploitation outside the citizen community depend on the existence of an exploited sub-citizen class, whether of slaves, women, or aliens?[71] Does increasing scale and/or economic efficiency inevitably mean declining social equality? Political scientists are fond of arguing that the Greek democratic experience has no relevance for the modern world.[72] That is clearly not the case. Despite the obvious differences, the modern world faces some of the same questions about the nature of a good society as did the classical Greeks.[73] The Greeks tackled them without benefit of historical understanding and without comparative analysis. We do not have to do the same; but whether we can do any better than the Athenians is another question altogether.

## Notes

1. Polanyi 1944; Polanyi, Arensberg, and Pearson 1957. On Polanyi's seminar group at Columbia see Polanyi and Arensberg 1957; Humphreys 1978, 38–45; Block and Somers 1984, 50–52; Dalton 1990.
2. The best summaries of the historiography are Will 1954 and Austin and Vidal-Naquet 1977, 3–8.
3. Polanyi 1977; 1957. The Aristotle passages are conveniently translated in Austin and Vidal-Naquet 1977, 162–68; 225–29. Lowry (1987, 182–212) reviews interpretations and explicates the texts.
4. See Humphreys 1978, 45–75; Austin and Vidal-Naquet 1977, 7–18; Lowry 1979; Meikle 1979; 1991; Nippel 1982; Hopkins 1983a; Andreau and Étienne 1984.
5. In many cases, the opposition stems from a misunderstanding, with historians casting substantivists merely as "primitivists" who oppose "modernist" exaggerations of the level of ancient trade and industrial activity: e.g., Harris 1988, 37, n. 81; E. Cohen 1992, 1–8. Burke (1992, 199–201) is more positive, but shares this view. For a clear statement, see Millett 1991, 9–16.
6. Finley 1952; 1954; 1974 [1970]. On Finley's relationship to Polanyi, see Finley 1975, 117; Humphreys 1978, 42–43; Shaw and Saller 1981, xix; Shaw 1993.
7. Finley 1974, 44.
8. Finley 1985; 1981, 176–95.
9. Justified in Ober 1989, 36–38; E. Cohen 1992, xiii; criticized in Morris forthcoming a.
10. See Hopkins 1978; 1980; 1983a; 1983b; Jongman 1990; Love 1991; with Finley's response to his critics at 1985, 177–206. The most extreme critique is Engels 1990, on which see Tompkins 1990; Saller 1991.
11. Morris forthcoming b.

12. On the other *politeiai*, see Weil 1960, 179–323; on Aristotle's empiricism, Whitehead 1991, 137–41.
13. On aristocratic orders, see, e.g., Powis 1984. MacKendrick (1969) does represent Athenian aristocrats as such an order, defined through membership of a *genos;* but Ober (1989, 104–18, 248–59) gives a more balanced view.
14. I set out my views on the archaic social transformations in Morris 1987; 1989; 1991; forthcoming c. On the importance of law, see, in differing ways, Ostwald 1986; Ober 1989; D. Cohen 1989; Todd and Millett 1990; and on sycophants, the opposed views of R. Osborne 1990; Harvey 1990.
15. For examples of all these criteria, see Aeschines 1.42; 3.11, 218; Demosthenes 21.183; 29.24; 54.15, 17; Dinarchus 2.8; Hyperides 4.21; Isaeus 7.40; Lysias fr. 73. I draw heavily here on the important discussion in Ober 1989, 257–59, and *passim*. On *homonoia*, see Funke 1980, 13–26; Ober 1989, 297–99; cf. 70–71.
16. The term comes from Sahlins 1972, 193–230. See Aristotle, *Ethics* 1157b35, 1158b11–59a5, 1171b32, with Millett 1991, 116–23.
17. Winkler 1990, 177.
18. Fisher 1992, 1; cf. Ober 1989, 208–210; forthcoming.
19. Fisher 1992, 493. See also D. Cohen 1991a; 1991b, for somewhat different views.
20. Halperin 1990, 99. On phalanx solidarity, see Hanson 1989, 123–25; on farming, Burford 1993, 28, 37.
21. On wealth distribution, see Davies 1981, 9–37; Rhodes 1982; Ober 1989, 127–31; R. Osborne 1992. On poor citizens, Ober 1989, 134–44; landless citizens, Jameson 1992, 144–45; suspension of disbelief, Ober 1989, 152–55; quotation from Halperin 1990, 103.
22. The exclusions are described in Just 1989; M. Osborne 1983. On the space of equality, see Sen 1992, 12–30; Cartledge forthcoming. Patterson (1986) argues that the geo-*polis* was more important than the politico-*polis;* for more critical views of such issues, see Okin 1991; Phillips 1991, 147–68; Mendus 1992.
23. See Adkins 1963.
24. Aristotle's terminology is fraught with dangers. Raaflaub (1983; 1985) examines the changes in the idea of the "free citizen" in the fifth century. On natural slavery, see Cambiano 1987; Schofield 1990.
25. Millett 1991. E. Cohen (1992) builds a sharply different model.
26. There is a large literature on the difficult issue of how far we can generalize from Aristotle. The differing views can be seen in Dover 1974, 1–25; Adkins 1978; Taylor 1990.
27. Loraux 1991, 34–35.
28. Gehrke (1985) argues that in the fifth and fourth centuries violence never arose from internal disputes among citizens, but only when another power sought to exploit civic disagreements through armed force.
29. Ste. Croix 1981, 69–80; Ober 1991.
30. On the problems, see Millett 1983, 37; Hansen 1984; E. Cohen 1990.
31. Hasebroek 1933.
32. E.g., Erxleben 1974. A fierce controversy has developed over the role of banking in the Athenian economy, and the extent to which Athenian banking was in citizen hands (see Millett 1991; E. Cohen 1992).

33. Bloch and Parry 1989, 26.
34. E.g., Bellah et al. 1985; 1991; Bowles and Gintis 1986.
35. See Garnsey 1988, 8–16; Garnsey and Morris 1989; Halstead 1989; Gallant 1991, 1–59.
36. Whitehead 1984.
37. On the disabilities of metics and their continued attachment to their home *poleis*, see Whitehead 1977; 1986.
38. Burke 1992, 208.
39. Finley 1980, 86–92; 1981, 167–75.
40. Finley 1981, 99–100, 115.
41. Ste. Croix 1981, 505–506; Lauffer 1979; Garlan 1988, 60–69.
42. Jameson 1978. On farm sizes, see Andreyev 1974; Burford-Cooper 1978; Alcock, Cherry, and Davis 1994, 160–64.
43. Wood 1983; 1988, 42–60.
44. R. Osborne 1988.
45. Wood 1988, 5–41.
46. Finley 1980, 11–66; Jameson 1992. On intensity, Halstead 1987; 1990; Alcock 1993, 49–72; Alcock, Cherry, and Davis 1994, 148–51. Generally, see Burford 1993, 208–222.
47. Cartledge 1985.
48. In this I disagree with Ste. Croix 1981, 98–111.
49. E.g., Keuls 1992; Bérard 1989.
50. Cartledge 1983; Bravo 1984.
51. Garnsey 1988, 8–119; Garnsey and Morris 1989; Morris 1991, 34–36. Sallares (1991, 96–97) would push the origins of dependency down to the late fifth century, but this is a genuinely primitivist argument.
52. For general accounts of the period, see Kagan 1969; Meiggs 1972; Rhodes 1985.
53. Finley 1981, 41–61; Millett 1989. Burke (1992, 215–25) has an interesting discussion of the impact of state pay.
54. Davies 1978, 76–98; Morris 1992a.
55. Kagan 1974, 17–42.
56. Kagan 1974, 144–46, 363–64.
57. Ober 1985a; 1985b, 32–50.
58. Cartledge 1979, 224–66; 1987, 34–54. On fifth-century Spartan finance, see Loomis 1992.
59. Hamilton 1979, 88–96; Bommelaer 1981, 223–38; Cartledge 1987, 93–98.
60. Cf. Ste. Croix 1953; Strauss 1986, 42–69; Burke 1990; Pritchett 1991, 480–504.
61. Rhodes 1980, 309–14; Cawkwell 1963; Will 1983, 48–100; Humphreys 1985; Burke 1985.
62. Rhodes 1980, 314–15; Garlan 1976, 93–103.
63. Morris 1992b, 128–55; forthcoming c. On houses, see Hoepfner and Schwandner 1986.
64. As argued at length by Mossé 1962; Welskopf 1974.
65. Ober 1989, 102; Millett 1991, 19–23; Finley 1974.
66. Ober 1991.
67. Strauss 1991, 229–33.

68. Chroust 1973, 83–176.
69. Runciman 1989, 326–36; 1990.
70. Ste. Croix 1981, 518–37. Bernhardt (1985) disputes this.
71. As implied by Walzer (1983, 52–63) in his comparison of Athenian metics and German *Gastarbeiter;* cf. Kennedy 1993, 82–94.
72. E.g., Holmes 1979, disputed by Euben 1990, 5–18.
73. Seen most clearly in the debates between communitarianists and liberals. See Bellah et al. 1991; Mulhall and Swift 1992; the papers in Avineri and de-Shalit 1992; Nussbaum and Sen 1993.

## References

Adkins, Arthur. 1963. "'Friendship' and 'Self-Sufficiency' in Homer and Aristotle." *Classical Quarterly* 13:30–45.
———. 1978. "Problems in Greek Popular Morality." *Classical Philology* 73:143–58.
Alcock, Susan E. 1993. *Graecia capta: The Landscapes of Roman Greece.* Cambridge: Cambridge University Press.
Alcock, Susan E., John F. Cherry, and Jack L. Davis. 1994. "Intensive Survey, Agricultural Practice, and the Classical Landscape of Greece." In *Classical Greece: Ancient Histories and Modern Archaeologies,* edited by Ian Morris, 137–70. Cambridge: Cambridge University Press.
Andreau, Jean, and Roland Étienne. 1984. "Vingt ans de recherches sur l'archaisme et la modernité des sociétés antiques." *Revue des études anciennes* 86:55–83.
Andreyev, V. N. 1974. "Some Aspects of Agrarian Conditions in Attica in the Fifth to Third Centuries B.C." *Eirene* 12:5–46.
Austin, Michel, and Pierre Vidal-Naquet. 1977. *Economic and Social History of Ancient Greece.* London: Batsford.
Avineri, Shlomo, and Avner de-Shalit, eds. 1992. *Communitarianism and Individualism.* Oxford: Oxford University Press.
Bellah, Robert N., Richard Madsen, William M. Sullivan, Ann Swidler, and Steven M. Tipton. 1985. *Habits of the Heart: Individualism and Commitment in American Life.* New York: Harper.
———. 1991. *The Good Society.* New York: Harper.
Bérard, Claude. 1989. "The Order of Women." In *The City of Images: Iconography and Society in Ancient Greece,* edited by Claude Bérard, Christiane Bron, Jean-Louis Durand, Françoise Frontisi-Ducroux, François Lissarrague, Alain Schnapp, and Jean-Pierre Vernant, 89–107. Princeton: Princeton University Press.
Bernhardt, R. 1985. *Polis und römische Herrschaft in der späten Republik, 149–31 v. Chr.* Berlin: de Gruyter.
Bloch, Maurice, and Jonathan Parry. 1989. Introduction: "Money and the Morality of Exchange." In *Money and the Morality of Exchange,* edited by Maurice Bloch and Jonathan Parry, 1–32. Cambridge: Cambridge University Press.

Block, Fred, and Margaret R. Somers. 1984. "Beyond the Economistic Fallacy: The Holistic Social Science of Karl Polanyi." In *Vision and Method in Historical Sociology*, edited by Theda Skocpol, 47–84. Cambridge: Cambridge University Press.
Bommelaer, Jean-François. 1981. *Lysandre de Sparte*. Paris: Les Belles Lettres.
Bowles, Samuel, and Herbert Gintis. 1986. *Democracy and Capitalism: Property, Community, and the Contradictions of Modern Social Thought*. New York: Basic Books.
Bravo, Benedetto. 1984. "Commerce et noblesse en Grèce archaïque." *Dialogues d'histoire ancienne* 10:99–160.
Burford, Alison. 1993. *Land and Labor in the Greek World*. Baltimore: Johns Hopkins University Press.
Burford-Cooper, Alison. 1978. "The Family Farm in Greece." *Classical Journal* 73:162–75.
Burke, Edmund M. 1985. "Lycurgan Finances." *Greek, Roman and Byzantine Studies* 26:251–64.
———. 1990. "Athens after the Peloponnesian War: Restoration Efforts and the Role of Maritime Commerce." *Classical Antiquity* 9:1–13.
———. 1992. "The Economy of Athens in the Classical Period: Some Adjustments to the Primitivist Model." *Transactions of the American Philological Association* 122:199–226.
Cambiano, Giuseppe. 1987. "Aristotle and the Anonymous Opponents of Slavery." In *Classical Slavery*, edited by Moses I. Finley, 21–41. London: George Cass (*Slavery and Abolition* 8).
Cartledge, Paul. 1979. *Sparta and Lakonia*. London: Routledge and Kegan Paul.
———. 1983. "'Trade and Politics' Revisited: Archaic Greece." In *Trade in the Ancient Economy*, edited by Peter Garnsey, Keith Hopkins, and C.R. Whittaker, 1–15. Cambridge: Cambridge University Press.
———. 1985. "Rebels and Sambos in Classical Greece: A Comparative View." In *Crux: Essays in Greek History Presented to G. E. M. de Ste. Croix*, edited by Paul Cartledge and F. David Harvey, 16–46. London: Duckworth (*History of Political Thought* 6).
———. 1987. *Agesilaos and the Crisis of Sparta*. London: Duckworth.
———. Forthcoming. "Comparatively Equal." In *Democracy Ancient and Modern*, edited by Charles Hedrick and Josiah Ober. Princeton: Princeton University Press.
Cawkwell, George. 1963. "Eubulus." *Journal of Hellenic Studies* 83:47–67.
Chroust, A.-H. 1973. *Aristotle: New Light on His Life and Some of His Lost Works*. London: Routledge and Kegan Paul.
Cohen, David. 1989. "Models and Methods in the Study of Greek Law." *Zeitschrift der Savigny-Stiftung, Romanistische Abteilung* 106:81–105.
———. 1991a. "Sexuality, Violence, and the Athenian Law of *Hybris*." *Greece and Rome* 38:171–88.
———. 1991b. *Law, Sexuality, and Society: The Enforcement of Morals in Classical Athens*. Cambridge: Cambridge University Press.
Cohen, Edward E. 1990. "Commercial Lending by Athenian Banks: Cliometric Fallacies and Forensic Methodology." *Classical Philology* 85:177–90.

———. 1992. *Athenian Economy and Society: A Banking Perspective*. Princeton: Princeton University Press.
Dalton, George. 1990. "Writings that Clarify Theoretical Disputes over Karl Polanyi's Work." In *The Life and Work of Karl Polanyi*, edited by Kari Polanyi-Levitt, 161–169. Montréal: Black Rose Books.
Davies, J. K. 1978. *Democracy and Classical Greece*. Glasgow: Fontana.
———. 1981. *Wealth and the Power of Wealth in Classical Athens*. New York: Arno.
Dover, K. J. 1974. *Greek Popular Morality in the Age of Plato and Aristotle*. Berkeley: University of California Press.
Engels, Donald. 1990. *Roman Corinth: An Alternative Model for the Classical City*. Chicago: University of Chicago Press.
Erxleben, E. 1974. "Die Rolle der Bevölkerungsklassen im Aussenhandel Athens im 4. Jahrhundert v. u. Z." In Welskopf 1974, 460–520.
Euben, Peter J. 1990. *The Tragedy of Political Theory: The Road Not Taken*. Berkeley: University of California Press.
Finley, Moses I. 1952. *Studies in Land and Credit in Ancient Athens*. New Brunswick: Rutgers University Press. Reissued New York: Arno Press, 1979; Cambridge: Cambridge University Press, 1985.
———. 1954. *The World of Odysseus*. New York: Viking.
———. 1974 [1970]. Aristotle and Economic Analysis. In *Studies in Ancient Society*, edited by Moses I. Finley. London: Routledge and Kegan Paul. First published in *Past and Present* 47 (1970):3–25.
———. 1975. *The Use and Abuse of History*. London: Chatto and Windus.
———. 1980. *Ancient Slavery and Modern Ideology*. London: Chatto and Windus.
———. 1981. *Economy and Society in Ancient Greece*, edited by Brent D. Shaw and Richard P. Saller. London: Chatto and Windus.
———. 1985. *The Ancient Economy*. 2d ed. London: Hogarth Press.
Fisher, Nicholas. 1992. *Hybris*. Warminster: Aris and Phillips.
Funke, Peter. 1980. *Homonoia und Arche*. Stuttgart: Steiner (*Historia* Einzelschrift).
Gallant, Thomas W. 1991. *Risk and Survival in Ancient Greece*. Stanford: Stanford University Press.
Garlan, Yvon. 1976. *War in the Ancient World: A Social History*. London: Chatto and Windus.
———. 1988. *Slavery in Ancient Greece*. Ithaca, NY: Cornell University Press.
Garnsey, Peter. 1988. *Famine and Food Supply in the Graeco-Roman World*. Cambridge: Cambridge University Press.
Garnsey, Peter, and Ian Morris. 1989. "Risk and the *polis*." In *Bad Year Economics*, edited by Paul Halstead and John O'Shea, 98–105. Cambridge: Cambridge University Press.
Gehrke, Hans-Joachim. 1985. *Stasis: Untersuchungen zu inneren Kriegen in den griechischen Staaten des 5. und 4. Jhs*. Stuttgart: C. H. Beck (*Vestigia* 35).
Halperin, David. 1990. *One Hundred Years of Homosexuality*. London: Routledge.
Halstead, Paul. 1987. "Traditional and Ancient Rural Economies in Mediterranean Europe: Plus ça change?" *Journal of Hellenic Studies* 107:77–87.
———. 1989. "The Economy Has a Normal Surplus: Economic Stability and Social Change among Early Farming Communities of Thessaly, Greece." In *Bad Year*

Economics, edited by Paul Halstead and John O'Shea, 68–80. Cambridge: Cambridge University Press.
———. 1990. "Waste Not, Want Not: Traditional Responses to Crop Failure in Greece." *Rural History* 1:147–64.
Hamilton, Charles. 1979. *Sparta's Bitter Victories*. Ithaca, NY: Cornell University Press.
Hansen, Marianne V. 1984. "Athenian Maritime Trade in the Fourth Century B.C.: Operation and Finance." *Classica et Medievalia* 35:71–92.
Hanson, Victor. 1989. *The Western Way of War: Infantry Battle in Classical Greece*. Oxford: Oxford University Press.
Harris, Edward M. 1988. "When Is a Sale Not a Sale? The Riddle of Athenian Terminology for Real Security Revisited." *Classical Quarterly* 38:39–41.
Harvey, F. David. 1990. "The Sycophant and Sycophancy: Vexatious Redefinition?" In *Nomos: Essays in Athenian Law, Politics and Society*, edited by Paul Cartledge, Paul Millett, and Stephen Todd, 103–121. Cambridge: Cambridge University Press.
Hasebroek, Johannes. 1933. *Trade and Politics in Ancient Greece*. London: Bell.
Hoepfner, Wolfram, and Ernst-Ludwig Schwandner. 1986. *Haus und Stadt im klassischen Griechenland*. Munich: Deutscher Kunstverlag.
Holmes, Stephen. 1979. "Aristippus In and Out of Athens." *American Political Science Review* 73:113–28.
Hopkins, M. Keith. 1978. "Economic Growth and Towns in Classical Antiquity." In *Towns in Societies*, edited by P. Abrams and E. A. Wrigley, 35–77. Cambridge: Cambridge University Press.
———. 1980. "Taxes and Trade in the Roman Empire (200 B.C.–A.D. 400)." *Journal of Roman Studies* 70:101–125.
———. 1983a. Introduction. In *Trade in the Ancient Economy*, edited by Peter Garnsey, Keith Hopkins, and C. R. Whittaker, ix–xxv. Cambridge: Cambridge University Press.
———. 1983b. "Models, Ships and Staples." In *Trade and Famine in Classical Antiquity*, edited by Pater Garnsey and C. R. Whittaker, 84–109. Cambridge: Proceedings of the Cambridge Philological Society, supp. vol. 8.
Humphreys, S. C. 1978. *Anthropology and the Greeks*. London: Routledge and Kegan Paul.
———. 1985. "Lycurgus of Butadae: An Athenian Aristocrat." In *The Craft of the Ancient Historian*, edited by John Eadie and Josiah Ober, 199–252. Lanham, MD: University Presses of America.
Jameson, Michael H. 1978. "Agriculture and Slavery in Classical Athens." *Classical Journal* 73:122–45.
———. 1992. "Agricultural Labor in Greece." In *Agriculture in Ancient Greece*, edited by Berit Wells, 135–46. Stockholm: Skrifter Utgivna i Svenska Institutet i Athen.
Jongman, W. 1988. *The Economy and Society of Pompeii*. Amsterdam: Hakkert.
Just, Roger. 1989. *Women in Athenian Law and Life*. London: Routledge.
Kagan, Donald. 1969. *The Outbreak of the Peloponnesian War*. Ithaca, NY: Cornell University Press.

———. 1974. *The Archidamian War*. Ithaca, NY: Cornell University Press.
Kennedy, Paul. 1993. *Preparing for the Twenty-First Century*. New York: Random House.
Keuls, Eva. 1992. *The Reign of the Phallus*. 2nd ed. Berkeley: University of California Press.
Lauffer, Siegfried. 1979. *Die Bergwerkssklaven von Laureion*. 2d ed. Wiesbaden: Steiner.
Loomis, William. 1992. *The Spartan War Fund*. Wiesbaden: Steiner (*Historia* Einzelschrift 74).
Loraux, Nicole. 1991. "Reflections of the Greek City on Unity and Division." In *City States in Classical Antiquity and Medieval Italy*, edited by Anthony Molho, Julia Emmen, and Kurt Raaflaub, 33–51. Stuttgart: Steiner.
Lowry, S. Todd. 1979. "Recent Literature in Ancient Greek Economic Thought." *Journal of Economic Literature* 17:65–86.
———. 1987. *The Archaeology of Economic Ideas: The Classical Greek Tradition*. Durham, NC: Duke University Press.
MacKendrick, Paul. 1969. *The Athenian Aristocracy, 399–31 B.C.* Cambridge, MA: Harvard University Press.
Meiggs, Russell. 1972. *The Athenian Empire*. Oxford: Clarendon Press.
Meikle, Scott C. 1979. "Aristotle and the Political Economy of the *Polis*." *Journal of Hellenic Studies* 99:57–73.
———. 1991. "Aristotle on Equality and Market Exchange." *Journal of Hellenic Studies* 111:193–96.
Mendus, Susan. 1992. "Losing the Faith: Feminism and Democracy." In *Democracy: The Unfinished Journey, 508 B.C. to A.D. 1993*, edited by John Dunn, 207–20. Oxford: Oxford University Press.
Millett, Paul. 1983. "Maritime Loans and the Structure of Credit in Fourth-Century Athens." In *Trade in the Ancient Economy*, edited by Peter Garnsey, Keith Hopkins, and C. R. Whittaker, 36–52. Cambridge: Cambridge University Press.
———. 1989. "Patronage and Its Avoidance in Classical Athens." In *Patronage in Ancient Society*, edited by Andrew Wallace-Hadrill, 1–33. London: Routledge.
———. 1991. *Lending and Borrowing in Ancient Athens*. Cambridge: Cambridge University Press.
Morris, Ian. 1987. *Burial and Ancient Society: The Rise of the Greek City-State*. Cambridge: Cambridge University Press.
———. 1989. "Circulation, Deposition, and the Formation of the Greek Iron Age." *Man* 24:502–19.
———. 1991. "The Early *Polis* as City and State." In *City and Country in the Ancient World*, edited by John Rich and Andrew Wallace-Hadrill, 24–57. London: Routledge.
———. 1992a. "Greeks on the Move." *Ancient History Bulletin* 6:137–45.
———. 1992b. *Death-Ritual and Social Structure in Classical Antiquity*. Cambridge: Cambridge University Press.
———. Forthcoming a. "Periodization." In *Inventing Ancient Culture*, edited by Peter Toohey and Mark Golden. London: Routledge.
———. Forthcoming b. *The Archaeology of Democracy*. Oxford: Basil Blackwell.

———. Forthcoming c. "The Strong Principle of Equality and the Archaic Origins of Greek Democracy." In *Democracy Ancient and Modern*, edited by Charles Hedrick and Josiah Ober. Princeton: Princeton University Press.
Mossé, Claude. 1962. *La Fin de la démocratie athénienne*. Paris: Les Belles Lettres.
Mulhall, Stephen, and Adam Swift. 1992. *Liberals and Communitarians*. Oxford: Basil Blackwell.
Nippel, Wilfried. 1982. "Die Heimkehr der Argonauten aus der Südsee. Ökonomische Anthropologie und die Theorie der griechischen Gesellschaft in klassischer Zeit." *Chiron* 12:1–39.
Nussbaum, Martha, and Amartya Sen, eds. 1993. *The Quality of Life*. Oxford: Oxford University Press.
Ober, Josiah. 1985a. "Thucydides, Pericles, and the Strategy of Defense." In *The Craft of the Ancient Historian*, edited by John Eadie and Josiah Ober, 171–88. Lanham, MD: University Presses of America.
———. 1985b. *Fortress Attica: The Defense of the Athenian Land Frontier, 404–322 B.C.* Leiden: Mnemosyne supp. 84.
———. 1989. *Mass and Elite in Democratic Athens: Rhetoric, Ideology, and the Power of the People*. Princeton: Princeton University Press.
———. 1991. "Aristotle's Political Sociology: Class, Status, and Order in the *Politics*." In *Essays on the Foundations of Aristotelian Political Science*, edited by Carnes Lord and David O'Connor, 112–35. Berkeley: University of California Press.
———. Forthcoming. "Oratory and Power in Democratic Athens: Demosthenes 21, Against Meidias." In *Greek Rhetoric: Influences and Influence*, edited by Ian Worthington. London: Routledge.
Okin, Susan M. 1991. "Gender, the Public and the Private." In *Political Theory Today*, edited by David Held, 67–90. Oxford: Polity Press.
Osborne, Michael J. 1983. *Naturalization at Athens* III/IV. Brussels: Paleis der Academiën.
Osborne, Robin. 1988. "Social and Economic Implications of the Leasing of Land and Property in Classical and Hellenistic Greece." *Chiron* 18:279–323.
———. 1990. "Vexatious Litigation in Classical Athens: Sykophancy and the Sykophant." In *Nomos: Essays in Athenian Law, Politics and Society*, edited by Paul Cartledge, Paul Millett, and Stephen Todd, 83–102. Cambridge: Cambridge University Press.
———. 1992. "'Is It a Farm?' The Definition of Agricultural Sites and Settlements in Ancient Greece." In *Agriculture in Ancient Greece*, edited by Berit Wells, 21–27. Stockholm: Skrifter Utgivna i Svenska Institutet i Athen.
Ostwald, Martin. 1986. *From Popular Sovereignty to the Sovereignty of Law*. Berkeley: University of California Press.
Patterson, Cynthia. 1986. "*Hai Attikai*: The Other Athenians." *Helios* 13:49–67.
Phillips, Anne. 1991. *Engendering Democracy*. University Park: Pennsylvania State University Press.
Polanyi, Karl. 1944. *The Great Transformation*. New York: Holt, Rinehart and Winston.
———. 1957. "Aristotle Discovers the Economy." In Polanyi, Arensberg, and Pearson 1957, 64–94.

———. 1977. *The Livelihood of Man*, edited by Harry W. Pearson. New York: Academic Press.
Polanyi, Karl, and Conrad M. Arensberg. 1957. "Preface." In Polanyi, Arensberg, and Pearson 1957, v–xi.
Polanyi, Karl, Conrad M. Arensberg, and Harry W. Pearson, eds. 1957. *Trade and Market in the Early Empires*. Glencoe, IL: Free Press.
Powis, Jonathan. 1984. *Aristocracy*. Oxford: Basil Blackwell.
Pritchett, W. Kendrick. 1991. *The Greek State at War V*. Berkeley: University of California Press.
Raaflaub, Kurt. 1983. "Democracy, Oligarchy, and the Concept of the 'Free Citizen' in Late Fifth-Century Athens." *Political Theory* 11:517–44.
———. 1985. *Die Entdeckung der Freiheit. Zur historischen Semantik und Gesellschaftsgeschichte eines politischen Grundbegriffs der Griechen*. Munich: C. H. Beck (*Vestigia* 37).
Rhodes, Peter J. 1980. "Athenian Democracy after 403 B.C." *Classical Journal* 75:305–23.
———. 1982. "Problems in Athenian *Eisphora* and Liturgies." *American Journal of Ancient History* 7:1–19.
———. 1985. *The Athenian Empire*. Oxford: *Greece and Rome* New Surveys in the Classics 17.
Runciman, W. Gary. 1989. *A Treatise on Social Theory II*. Cambridge: Cambridge University Press.
———. 1990. "Doomed to Extinction? The *Polis* as an Evolutionary Dead End." In *The Greek City from Homer to Alexander*, edited by Oswyn Murray and Simon Price, 347–67. Oxford: Oxford University Press.
Sahlins, Marshall D. 1972. *Stone Age Economics*. Chicago: Aldine.
Ste. Croix, G. E. M. de. 1953. "Demosthenes' *Timema* and the Athenian *Eisphora* in the Fourth Century B.C." *Classica et Medievalia* 14:30–70.
———. 1981. *The Class Struggle in the Ancient Greek World*. London: Duckworth.
Sallares, Robert. 1991. *The Ecology of the Ancient Greek World*. London: Duckworth.
Saller, Richard P. 1991. Review of Engels 1990. *Classical Philology* 86:351–57.
Schofield, Malcolm. 1990. "Ideology and Philosophy in Aristotle's Theory of Slavery." In *Aristoteles "Politik": Akten des XI. Symposium Aristotelicum*, edited by Gunther Patzig, 1–27. Göttingen: Vandenhoeck und Ruprecht.
Sen, Amartya. 1992. *Inequality Reexamined*. Cambridge, MA: Harvard University Press.
Shaw, Brent D. 1993. "The Early Development of M. I. Finley's Thought: The Heichelheim Dossier." *Athenaeum* 81:177–99.
Shaw, Brent D., and Richard P. Saller. 1981. "Editors' Introduction." In Finley 1981, ix–xxvi.
Strauss, Barry. 1986. *Athens after the Peloponnesian War: Class, Faction, and Policy, 403–386 B.C*. Ithaca, NY: Cornell University Press.
———. 1991. "On Aristotle's Critique of Athenian Democracy." In *Essays on the Foundations of Aristotelian Political Science*, edited by Carnes Lord and David O'Connor, 212–33. Berkeley: University of California Press.

Taylor, Charles. 1990. "Popular Morality and Unpopular Philosophy." In *Owls to Athens: Essays Presented to Sir Kenneth Dover*, edited by Elizabeth Craik, 233–43. Oxford: Oxford University Press.
Todd, Stephen, and Paul Millett. 1990. "Law, Society and Athens." In *Nomos: Essays in Athenian Law, Politics and Society*, edited by Paul Cartledge, Paul Millett, and Stephen Todd, 1–18. Cambridge: Cambridge University Press.
Tompkins, Daniel P. 1990. Review of Engels 1990. *Bryn Mawr Classical Review* 1:20–33.
Walzer, Michael. 1983. *Spheres of Justice: A Defense of Pluralism and Equality*. New York: Basic Books.
Weil, Raymond. 1960. *Aristote et l'histoire: essai sur la Politique*. Paris: Les Belles Lettres.
Welskopf, Elisabeth, ed. 1974. *Hellenische Poleis*. 4 vols. Berlin: Akademie-Verlag.
Whitehead, David. 1977. *The Ideology of the Athenian Metic*. Cambridge: Proceedings of the Cambridge Philological Society, supp. vol. 4.
———. 1984. "Immigrant Communities in the Classical *Polis*." *L'Antiquité classique* 53:47–59.
———. 1986. "The Ideology of the Athenian Metic: Some Pendants and a Reappraisal." *Proceedings of the Cambridge Philological Society* n.s. 31:145–58.
———. 1991. "Norms of Citizenship in Ancient Greece." In *City States in Classical Antiquity and Medieval Italy*, edited by Anthony Molho, Julia Emmen, and Kurt Raaflaub, 133–54. Stuttgart: Steiner.
Will, Edouard. 1954. "Trois quarts de siècle de recherches sur l'économie grecque antique." *Annales: économies, sociétés, civilisations* 9:7–22.
Winkler, John J. 1990. "Laying Down the Law: The Oversight of Men's Sexual Behavior in Classical Athens." In *Before Sexuality*, edited by David Halperin, John J. Winkler, and Froma I. Zeitlin, 171–210. Princeton: Princeton University Press.
Wood, Ellen Meiksens. 1983. "Agricultural Slavery in Classical Athens." *American Journal of Ancient History* 8:1–47.
———. 1988. *Peasant-Citizen and Slave*. London: Verso.

# 4

# The Institutional Theory of Trade and the Organization of Intersocial Commerce In Ancient Athens[*]

## John Adams

> Persons working on valued things, moving them and passing them from hand to hand, must, regardless of the relative scarcity or abundance of the things, know the rules of authority, and the rights and obligations in regard to the productive use of persons and things, and the rules of distribution of things; the cadences of work; the measures of time, weight, and space without which chaos would result. These are problems of the social, cultural, and physical dimensions of the substantive economy, and cannot be understood simply in terms of the abstraction, economizing on the use of scarce means, or "avoiding waste and futility."
>
> *Harry W. Pearson*[1]

### The Institutional Theory of Trade

Karl Polanyi's analysis of how long-distance trade articulates with the internal economic arrangements of societies ranks among his most powerful and creative contributions. He stressed the political character of such trade and its typical reliance on administrative control. Despite the potency of this theory, it has been neither ex-

---

[*] *The first version of this paper was read at the Third International Karl Polanyi Conference, held in Milan in November 1990.*

tended nor widely applied to actual cases. This chapter elaborates Polanyi's principles by adducing an admixture of American institutionalism and modern neoinstitutionalism. This amalgamation yields a theory of intersocial exchange that is more comprehensive and universal than the conventional neoclassical comparative-cost model. When applied to one of Polanyi's favourite historical exemplars, classical Athens, the theory generates new explanations of the Athenians' intentions and instruments.

Comparative advantage theory is inadequate because it concentrates almost entirely on supply costs, while neglecting consumption and the institutional arrangements that bring the exchanging parties together and permit them to consummate their transaction. It is most obviously limited by its assumption of frictionless markets in which fully informed agents share beliefs and commercial practices. According to this theory, international trade is driven by commercially oriented traders who operate in a fully developed global market system on the basis of private profit. All parties function in a contract-based milieu with zero enforcement costs. As the modifier "international" suggests, the nation is usually taken to be the trading and accounting unit.

Whatever their validity for modern times, these features render the theory unsuitable for scrutinizing ancient exchange patterns such as the Athenian trade in grains. This type of commerce was demand-based, generated by the lack of particular resources or commodities in the orbit of the domestic economy. Sufficiency and provisioning were the motives, not gain or profit; indeed, neither the State nor the individual had any basis for calibrating what we would today call balance of payments, terms of trade, or balance-sheet earnings. In addition to meeting social needs, goods often took the form of prestige items — tokens of rank or for use in sacred ceremonies. Markets were largely absent, as were commercial traders; exchange was episodic, keyed to cycles of weather, need, and ritual. The trading constituency was the society or community as a whole, politically organized as an empire or city-state, one function of which was to ensure adequate flows of primary commodities for mass use and of ceremonial goods for display purposes. The various societies had widely disparate systems of property rights, views of trade and traders, and means of regulating intersocial transactions. The insecurity of goods and agents in transit, when they moved in unsheltered limbo between the perimeters of the several trading communities, was a severe inhibition to trade. The lack of shared principles for enforcing agreements and resolving disputes was another chronic and costly handicap.

To Polanyi, intersocial movements of goods (trade) and monies (payments) take place through instituted processes.[2] This emphasis on the institutional and processual basis for trade in no way ignores geographical features engendering trade based on climate, soil, timberlands, or minerals. The point is that such "natural advantages," as Adam Smith called them, must be realized by the establishment of mutually acceptable institutional arrangements. Once in place, such arrangements facilitate exchanges by private agencies, such as family firms, or by public instruments, such as official trading parties. As for advancing the trade in goods, these institutionalized formations must solve two sets of problems. First, people from different social systems must devise a mode of trading that both enables the required goods to move and legitimizes the transfer of ownership at some particular place and moment; these are the locational and appropriational aspects of exchange. Second, such trade must permit goods and the agents bearing them to leave one society and enter another without undermining domestic economic and social relationships, including hierarchies of wealth and status.

## The Port of Trade

A common way of managing trade in primitive and ancient societies was the port of trade. Arnold defines the port of trade as an organ of administered trade, a way of trading which appears in general almost to the threshold of modern times. The capacity of the port of trade for outlasting the millennia reflected the positive role played by the institution in resolving some of the less obvious problems of statecraft under archaic conditions, such as military requirements and protection against undesirable cultural contact.[3]

At ports of trade the state became involved in many forms of regulation: the ratios of exchange between pairs of goods, or goods and monies; the security of persons and of property; the scheduling of trading activities; the construction of facilities; the establishment of weights and measures. According to Polanyi, ports of trade share three features: "economic administration, political neutrality, and ease of transportation."[4] Islands, oases, peninsulas, and mountain strongholds offered characteristics that frequently made them sites for ports of trade. Although Arnold says that the port of trade is not a modern form, many countries today rely upon export zones to facilitate linkages to the outside economy. The usual pattern is that a government that is not heavily market-oriented will establish a special estate or enclave in which the normal rules for export, investment, and foreign participation are attenuated or suspended, so that the nation can participate in the global market system without jeopardizing internal price relationships, tax requirements, or investment limitations.

In *Dahomey and the Slave Trade* Polanyi describes the emergence of Whydah as a port of trade in which slaves were exchanged for European coins or goods. In the late 1600s the volumes of gold and slaves swapped were small, being limited by the inability of the trading parties to construct a common institutional platform. Polanyi states wryly: "In effect, the European-chartered companies had no native partners to trade with, nor consequently trade agreements to live up to. Miscarried diplomatic contacts, abortive initiatives, sometimes ludicrous *contretemps* were the order of the day."[5] After 1704, Whydah functioned as a port of trade with forts established by the French, English, and Dutch, who committed themselves to neutrality and set — one may say conspired to fix — the terms of exchange. On the African side, the royal seat of government was Savi and the Houedan monarchy and its officials regulated local commerce and enforced order. The Europeans acknowledged the role of the king in mediating the flows of trade and setting the formulas for etiquette; gifts were designed to unite the two sides in common ceremony.

Conquest by the Dahomeans did not change the situation fundamentally, although the vicissitudes of local wars and the trans-Atlantic slave trade continually impinged upon Whydah and challenged the stability of arrangements there. As a port of trade, Whydah illustrates the importance of political control of the marketplace and the function of intermediation between two sharply contrasting institutional and normative regimes, both of which stood to make significant gains from exchange — once it could be satisfactorily ordered. The arrangements that were designed successfully partly realized those gains, which were based on the differing needs of the two disparate social systems and on underlying differences in production conditions and factor returns. For Athens, Peiraeus served as a weak port of trade, not as a rigorously bounded zone but as one that housed foreign traders, moneylenders, and maritime courts, in addition to the physical facilities of a bustling port. In their dealings with trading partners in the Mediterranean and Black seas, the Athenians did not emphasize the port of trade as a means of bridging cultural differences and reconciling different domestic exchange regimes; they chose to extend their own practices, with the effect of homogenizing commercial deportment on a foundation of shared values — an option that was open to them by virtue of their influence over the region and their unrivalled cultural achievements.

## Institutions and Trade

Although the port of trade is but one form of mediation between cultural and economic systems, the case of Whydah does illustrate the problems involved and the means by which these may be resolved. Looked at institutionally, archaic transcultural dealing has four common elements: 1) The motive for trade is to remedy a perceived need for food, war goods, luxuries, and status symbols. 2) There is a differentiation between the domestic and external spheres of exchange in organization, normative weight, and activating agencies. 3) Politics and Statecraft are the instruments through which exchange is motivated, stabilized, and monitored. The terms of exchange are heavily influenced by the comparative power and status of the involved parties. 4) Underlying geographical and supply conditions acquire salience only to the extent that they are actuated by institutional processes.

The institutional analysis of intersocial trade results in five propositions, as follows:[6]

*The more similar their institutions of exchange, the more intensively will two societies trade with each other.* Allowing for distance and other transport-cost factors, such as state infrastructure and the absence of politically motivated embargoes, it is a strong prediction of the theory that societies having analogous domestic exchange practices will trade in proportionately larger volumes. It is easier and less costly for agents of exchange to consummate transactions when rules are familiar to all parties. Shared language, monies, contract forms, weights and measures, enforcement procedures and remedies, and other dimensions of commercial practice will lower transaction costs. On the first point, language, it is easy to accede that the world's major trading regions either adopted a major tongue, such as English, or evolved pidgin dialects that spread along commercial pathways. Taking these elements together, the more they are dispersed, the more greatly is trade encouraged. This principle underpins the implementation of modern common markets or free-trade associations, which strive to homogenize their practices even as they retain or increase their differentiation from the outside world.

The converse corollary is: *The more divergent the exchange systems, the more difficult and costly the arranging of trade (and other transactions) and the lower the volume of exchange.* Effecting transactions between people with widely differing cultures, languages, and domestic exchange systems is costly, as Polanyi commented in discussing Whydah. When the breakdown is acute, war and plunder replace peace and commerce. The Age of Explorations is dotted with instances of mutual unintelligibility, most famously illustrated in the sale of Manhattan Island for twenty-four dollars worth of trade goods — a "sale" that had no pertinence to one party to the transaction and was certainly the source of as much mirth on one side as the other.

*World or regional trade expands more quickly as exchange systems become more similar.* During periods of increasing convergence of exchange systems, trade will grow more rapidly. When values and institutions become similar across exchange regimes, trade will swell, because communications, understanding, and the ability to bargain on common ground are enhanced. This proposition is of particular importance in the Athenian case, as will be demonstrated below. In the modern era, two periods of exceptional trade growth, 1870–1914 and 1950–1980, are marked by rapid extension of the global market system and its supporting property-right and institutional basis. Both witnessed rising international interdependence in all its forms. In the era after World War II, the role of the World Bank, the International Monetary Fund, and the General Agreement on Tariffs and Trade was central. In the earlier period, the gold standard and the balance-of-power system, both of which pivoted on the hegemonic role of England, were indispensable props, as Polanyi contended in *The Great Transformation*.[7]

To increase its intersocial transactions, a society must bring its exchange practices into harmony, if not exact conformity, with prevalent institutional practices. If a society wants to export or import more goods or services it must make adjustments to its institutional matrix. It may choose special forms — for example, in early times the port of trade; in more recent times the mercantile trading company or the modern state-trading corporation. It may adopt more or less wholesale the transactional forms of the other states with which it seeks to engage in external commerce, as Japan has done. The recent revolutions in Eastern Europe and the Soviet Union illustrate the risks and advantages of following this path, inevitable as it had become by 1990. The loss of state control was implied by the shift to a market-based exchange regime. The cases of China and India, two large nations with the potential for considerable self-reliance and low national export/output ratios, illustrate the chronic tensions and policy gyrations associated with trying to resolve the economic and political questions of joining the dominant global system of the late twentieth century. Lurking in the background in these old societies, and in the Islamic world, is the even more basic question of the degree to which cultural changes resulting from exposure to Western institutions for trade, travel, investment, and communications will influence values and lifestyles.

*Societies will follow their own methods of exchange, and extend these methods to other societies, when their power and influence enable them to do so.* In order to facilitate exchange and realize the aims of external transactions at lower costs, strong societies will attempt to project their own codes and practices into other milieux. This may be the result of either ignorance or disregard. The power of the Athenians lay in ships. In more recent centuries power has often been based on new weapons technologies. In cases ancient and modern, power is the force behind such institutional imperialism. Power can also be based on knowledge. Careful public and private record-keeping could provide an edge with respect to external commerce. Some of the early systematic bookkeeping of greatest interest to economic historians was done by bankers, merchant guilds, trading families, and commercial associations. It is not surprising that the first modern economic concept, the balance of trade, and the first national account, the balance of payments, date from the early days of the European mercantilists, who used such information to formulate and adjudge nation-building policies. The Greeks did not develop novel national or business accounts, but it is noteworthy that the Athenians' registers of payments of tribute from their city-state clients are an outstanding example of record-keeping in an otherwise insouciantly innumerate society. Furthermore, the object of immediate concern was the volume of wheat imports, given the goal of ensuring adequate food stocks. Crude warehouse benchmarks — how full are the sheds? — and the public mood were sufficient to monitor the state of affairs, which was equally an affair of state.

What is most important in developing an imperial commercial system is the ability to use power to insist that transactions be conducted according to one's own rules, that one's own coinage be employed, and that records be kept in a common accounting system. Influential societies impose on alien subjects their own views of property rights, contract law, treaty-agreement, and commercial codes. In this general fashion, imperialism may be seen as the imposition of new forms of exchange, and the institutions that foster and sustain them, on weaker, less-than-willing peoples. This imposition of alien modes substantially lowers transaction costs: the agents of the more powerful entity need not learn how to operate in a cumbersome or even primitive system. When colonies mirror the values and social organization of the mother culture there results a relatively direct way of tapping into resources and a simple way of arranging exchange relationships in a new or hostile world. The British dependencies in North America and the Spanish territories in South America illustrate this effective, low-cost means of opening up resources in a new world. It was easier and less costly to trade with confreres, even if they were cantankerous or independence-minded, than to truck with disparate and ignorant pre-commercial indigenous multitudes.

### The Athenian Thalassocracy

During the fifth century B.C., Athens experienced an unprecedented cultural efflorescence that does not need recounting here. During this classical period, Athenian power at its zenith extended throughout the central and eastern Mediterranean and into the Black Sea area. Tightly linked with the flourishing of the arts and with maritime influence was the importation of cereals. The city proper could not feed itself, nor could it create the monuments it coveted, without a mechanism to import grain. Agricultural production in the hinterland was insufficient to provide the brute energy needed for such endeavours as constructing temples, fortifying the city, and maintaining the fleet.[8] It was thus necessary to secure reliable sources of food for the population. In addition to meeting daily nutritional needs, inflows of food were required so that the Athenians and their slave-workers could construct tangible and lasting testaments to their grand collective urges. Put simply, our eyes mislead us: the temples on the Acropolis are built of wheat, not stone.

The chronology and major events in the rise of Athens to imperial glory are well-known; outlining them, however, will provide a structure for the argument that follows. The Greeks defeated the Persian fleet near Salamis in 480 B.C. This victory, and others in 479 and 478, saved Athens and the other Greek cities from the immediate Persian threat to their autonomy. In 477, the Delian League grouped Athens and most of the far-flung city-states in an alliance intended to stymie any future Persian resurgence. Sparta was alienated by the emergence of Athenian hegemony, and tensions mounted between the two cities and their respective allies. The two cities went to war in 431. Athens' allies in the Delian League paid substantial tribute, and filled other obligations, such as providing manned warships, to the leading city. Under the leadership of Pericles, Athenian influence radiated to the Black Sea, Egypt, Sicily, and southern Italy. The Athenian sphere had become more than a defensive shield fending off the Persians, for not by coincidence each of these areas produced large quantities of grain and shipped them to Athens. By 425, the League encompassed no fewer than 400 city-states.

### Athenian Public Finance

The precariousness of the Athenians' economic position in the fifth century cannot be exaggerated. Polanyi believed that while the Athenians are commonly recognized for the originality of their architecture and for their contributions to drama, the arts, and philosophy, it is equally important that we acknowledge the ingenuity with which they organized their public life, regulated their external economic relations, and governed domestic material transactions.[9] Their substantive economic organization was requisite for their cultural achievements, but in turn their cultural hubris was critical to their economic domination.

Goldsmith has provided a useful summation of Athenian public finance in the age of Pericles.[10] Attica's population of perhaps 320,000 comprised one-third slaves, one-fifth metics (resident foreigners) and freedmen, and just about one-half citizens (that is, male citizens plus members of their families). The population was about evenly divided between the countryside and the urban areas of Athens and Peiraeus. Only about seven percent of the citizens belonged to the two upper classes, the *pentakosiomedimnoi* and the *hippeis*, the remainder forming the third and fourth classes, the *zeugitai* and the *thetes*. The population grew because of natural increase and immigration, although mortality was high and variable and emigration considerable. Even with stagnant technology and an essentially fixed quantity of land, total output rose (although average output was probably only a little more than static). What is striking about the Athenian economy is the high ratio of economically unproductive public property, about one-eighth of the national wealth. Stocks of precious metals were an unusually large component of assets.[11] Both these anomalies can be explained by the heavy flow of tribute or dues entailed in the transfer of wealth from the periphery to the centre of the Athenian imperial dominion. Tribute amounted to about ten percent of national income.

Although the Athenians did not think in terms of a public budget, there is sufficient information to permit a partial modern reconstruction. Over half of the city's revenue came from the Delian confederation. Other sources of revenue were the silver mines at Laureion, income from state lands, and taxes on metics and slaves. Customs revenues and various excises were of some consequence; generally, taxes were farmed out. Two special obligations were placed on the heads of families of the elite classes: liturgy-supported festivals and public events. The trierarchy, a good example of a specialty liturgy, entailed the maintenance of a warship for one year. These redistributive obligations consumed a large share of the wealth of these honoured families, and they appear to have been accepted because of an almost unfathomable — to modern minds — sense of civic duty, probably combined with fears of ostracism and ridicule, the effective sanctions familiar to us from small-scale societies. Public works and naval and other military expenditures were the chief areas of spending. Welfare, religious, and political expenditures were heavy — perhaps "20,000 citizens or nearly one-half of all adult males received payment from the state."[12]

Goldsmith has assembled some credible numbers about Athenian exports and imports. It is striking that Athens produced almost nothing for export, in sharp contradistinction to medieval or modern cities. Domestic grain production, largely barley, met only about a quarter of the city's food requirements. Grain imports, mainly wheat, were therefore three times as great and had a calculable annual value of 700 talents in a total import "bill" of 1,000 talents. Slave imports may be assigned a total of seventy talents. The remaining import talents comprised mainly timber, iron, copper, hides, and luxury items.[13] As with most societies, Athens revealed its unmet needs through its imports: foodstuffs, slaves, war goods, and totems, each a hallmark of an aspect of Greek life. Exports totalled only a tiny fraction of imports — in modern terms, the balance of trade was in egregious deficit. This imbalance was covered, as it must always be, by a variety of non-product items, the largest of which was the confederacy tribute of 600 talents. Other invisibles were critical. Athens was an entrepôt, collecting shipping receipts. Athens and Peiraeus received income from tourism, pilgrimages, prostitution, and money-changing.[14]

Although it is possible to quibble with Goldsmith's public and trade accounts, and to doubt the validity of applying modern schemes to the ancient world, his general depiction of the patterns involved is useful. It demonstrates the fundamental weaknesses of the Athenian productive base, especially in agriculture, the tenuous nature of the public revenue relative to expenditure commitments, and the reliance on cereal imports. It is plain from the interpretations of Goldsmith and others that in order to flourish the Athenians had to create a number of institutions that would permit the elite to live very comfortably, ensure military dominance, and lay the foundation for a rich artistic and intellectual life. These social themes interlocked and reinforced one another; the absence or weakness of one would have undermined the others. Slavery was vital, but so were the panoply of practices centred on the *polis,* and participation in and service to it. On the economic and military fronts, the maritime strength of the city was irreducible and permitted the recruitment of tribute, which was in effect transferred through the grain trade. In turn, the organization of the inward flows of cereals and war goods was requisite for the maintenance of the fleet and for the sustenance of the city's work force and elite.

## The Institutionalization of the Grain Trade

Slavery, the *polis,* and the military basis of the Athenian thalassocracy are acknowledged facets of Athens society and economy. Less understood, even misunderstood, is the fourth pillar: the organization of the cereals commerce. The contours of the economy, the city's public finance, and the central position of the grain trade convey with compelling vividness the principles of the institutional theory of intersocial exchange. The codification and expression of these principles at the beginning of this chapter permit a fresh interpretation of Athenian circumstances. Above all, what is exemplified is the utility and generality of Polanyi's vision of intersocial trade as an instituted process. The Athenians brought ingenuity and creativity to bear in formulating their external exchange relations. As was the case with so many facets of life, their advances on this front conformed to timeless scientific and social principles, even as they inspired future awe and appreciation.

First in importance is the homogeneity or compatibility of institutional arrangements across trading partners. In this instance Athens was the core partner; the other was an allied city or colony. Generalized commercial practices involving money, markets, and credit were largely non-existent at this early moment in the history of the Mediterranean basin. Since a market system did not knit the cities together, it was necessary to rely upon non-market means. This is not to say that there were no market links, but these were not sufficient in and of themselves to coordinate the grain trade and meet the needs of Athens; nor were the Athenians predisposed to prorogate the market as their preferred mode of exchange. They therefore used a mixture of other devices, political and cultural — really, cultural, political, and economic all at once — in order to bring goods and resources into the centre of the League, from which devolved sufficient military force to ensure a measure of tranquillity in its domains. This overarching paradigm of exchange conforms, of course, to Polanyi's redistributive mode, with its multifarious bilateral connections and centrist focus.

An initially puzzling feature of Athenian trade is the degree to which Athens fostered the settlement of its citizens around the Mediterranean. Market-guided trade would have yielded goods movements as an easy substitute for the reduction in population. This emigration appears to have been a costly and unnecessary practice wasteful of the city's human resources. Why couldn't the Athenians merely exchange products or services on the basis of comparative-cost advantage with farmer-producers of whatever ethnicity in all of the many wheat-producing regions ringing the Mediterranean Sea?

The answer follows from an application of the theory of intersocial exchange, and it is threefold. First, there was no market system to organize such trade. Not only was the institution simply not known, but there was no intellectual and normative basis for it — the Athenian disdain for petty commerce, money-changing, and market-acquired wealth is widely and vigorously recorded; nor, for that matter, were the elite much enamoured of work as a source of income. Second, regulated quasi-market trade, and market agents *(emporoi)*, were relied upon, and although the agents were metics and foreigners they were given a degree of grudging respect for their contributions to the provisioning of the town. To allow even these limited forms of market exchange they had to be founded to the greatest extent possible on common units of coinage, standard numeraires, and widely pervasive weights and measures. In addition, commercial agreements or contracts had to be standardized and disputes had to be resolved in a consistent fashion. Third, non-market arrangements, through which the bulk of grain and other resources flowed to Athens, depended upon shared and mutually intelligible understandings between the Athenians and their suppliers. When seen as a pattern, this mixture of cultural, quasi-market, and administrative elements accounts for the brilliant successes of fifth-century

Athenian economy and society. Many apparently anomalous practices become intelligible when placed in the context of this pattern. Although the historical record is scant, it is plain that the Athenian alliance was based on a shared Hellenic civilization. The Athenians took measures to spread their culture and thus laid a foundation for mutual participation in a pattern of exchange that was substantially to their advantage. Their task was to lower the costs of empire and increase the benefits, in order to make the gathering of tribute as easy and as smooth as possible. The shared beliefs created a climate in which the pain of transferring grain and other goods to Athens was assuaged by intangible gains in the form of shared values, rituals, and lifestyles. Some cities were very close to Athens in this sense, some less so, others distant. Those which accepted the Athenian order willingly could be managed by diplomacy and by visits from roving commissioners *(episkopoi)*. Others required small garrisons under the command of a military commissioner *(phrourarchos)* or permanent supervisors *(archontes)*. Athenian aims were complex, but they included securing the peace, keeping the League together, and ensuring the transfer of the annual dues on which the city depended. Force and coercion were rarely employed and there was a bias towards local popular democracy, a tendency to base exchange on mutual interest and common accord rather than subjugation. Reports Meiggs: "Spartan behaviour in the Aegean when she attempted to take Athens' place provided a sharp contrast which Athenian orators appreciated: 'The Lacedaemonians put more men arbitrarily to death in three months than we brought to trial in the whole course of our empire'."[15]

The reliance on promulgating a shared culture, based on the philosophical and religious values of Athens, was not the only means of controlling the costs associated with the grain trade. The creation of settlements on uninhabited or lightly settled lands on the shores of the Mediterranean was another component of the Athenian design, predicated as it was on establishing points of grain production from which flows could be attracted to the core city. The cost superiority of seaborne trade over land trade was great, but the advantages of settler communities extended beyond this factor. Where communities already existed, but loyalty to Athens was weak, the placement of settlers strengthened the attachment of colonies *(cleruchies)*. Thus were engendered the shared understandings and institutions upon which Athenian dominance rested and, more narrowly, upon which the flow of grain was based. The hiving off of new colonies and the institution of *cleruchies* immediately established common cultural and economic denominators; dealing with purely non-Hellenes would have made exchange much more costly and problematic. Even if citizens and workers were lost to the hinterland from Athens, the gains from their transfer exceeded the losses involved in keeping them at home.

In the absence of sufficiently productive domestic agriculture and crafts to generate the requisite exportables, Athens could not sustain equal exchange with its external domains. It had neither the land, manpower, nor esteem of physical labour that might have made a more balanced exchange feasible. Force is the word most commonly used to explain the solidarity of the empire and Athens' ability to maintain the influx of food tribute it needed to survive. Yet the records show that coercion and punishment were rarely applied. It would have been hard to apply sustained extortion over the vast reaches of the empire. Other, more subtle explanations are more plausible. The exported grandeur of Athenian civilization, in its material and non-material manifestations, better served to balance its trade accounts than would have the discharge of menial effort in the making of commonplace products.

The colonists and clients who looked to Athens as a beacon felt a commitment to its values and its achievements. Pilgrimages were common and tourism flourished. Coming from a society in which trierarchies and liturgies were an established means of fulfilling social obligations, the settlers and dependents saw the unrequited transfer of cereals as a means of discharging their duties and obligations. This parallel has been little discussed. There is evidence of how this sense of attachment was cultivated. The Athenians honoured their friends in other cities by conferring on them the title of *proxenos* and exhibiting their names on stelae. Much was made of the cult of Athena and other embodiments of religious practice. When the colonial emissaries arrived with their annual tributary payments, they were feted — taken to plays and other entertainments. It was important that the residents of the confederation felt they belonged to a great cultural sphere, the radiating impulses of Athens at the centre ennobling its diverse components.

In his book on sea power in ancient history, Starr describes the administration of the empire in plausible terms but is unable to discern a reason for the consolidation of judicial authority in Athens. On the surface, to be sure, the centralization of legal authority would seem to be costly, since it required movement over long distances. It was potentially unjust, since local justices would have had access to testimony and precedent, as well as superior knowledge of the conditions surrounding the alleged malfeasance. Starr remarks: "In various degrees the independence of local courts was trimmed to require that capital penalties (death, exile, loss of public rights) could be inflicted only by Athenian juries — as the Old Oligarch observed, this was good for the Athenian hotel business."[16] Starr's attempt at humour conceals befuddlement, since he apparently fails to see that the intent was to standardize rules and procedures in criminal and civil law. Homogenization would in turn cut the costs of long-distance transactions and ease the burden of enforcement.

The institutional theory predicts that an imperial state will make a conscious effort to consolidate and universalize commercial practices. It would therefore be surprising if Athens had not formulated and attempted to impose a maritime code. In a pathbreaking study, Edward Cohen has traced the rise of Athenian maritime law and jurisprudence, including its centralization in Athens and Peiraeus.

Such a code was indispensable to the management and stimulation of the grain trade. The courts usually met to resolve disputes during the off-season. Not much of Greek law has survived to the present day but, interestingly enough, Athenian maritime principles are the "germinal cells" of modern international commercial codes.[17] In addition to creating a uniform civil, criminal, and maritime code, the Athenian elite devoted considerable attention to legislation governing the trade in grain and the deportment of its agents. Numerous acts were passed, especially in the fourth century when the Athenian empire was being reconstituted with even less reliance on force. Laws prohibited the extension of credit by citizens or resident metics for shipments to destinations other than Athens. Limits were put on the amount of grain that could be handled, usually by metic-agents, at any one time. Magistrates *(sitophylakes)* and inspectors *(epimeletai emporiou)* supervised the grain trade in the port and in Athens. No other commodity was so regulated.[18]

In their excellent study of the economic and social history of ancient Greece, which is heavily influenced by Polanyi's ideas, Austin and Vidal-Naquet appear puzzled by the Athenian effort of the fifth century to impose its coinage and system of weights and measures on the empire. "This was probably a political move in the first instance," they say, "rather than any sort of 'economic' or 'commercial' imperialism ...."[19] In their appended compendium of original sources they again confess to seeing no economic motive and further state that any benefit would be enjoyed by Athenians and non-Athenians alike.[20] Of course, this is precisely the point. Nothing would have suited Athenian interests better around the Mediterranean, within and outside their own immediate sphere of domination, than acceptance of their money and standards of weights and measures. Such unanimity would have harmonized their trading practices and facilitated their every effort at accountancy and exchange. The records are fragmentary but it is evident that Athens made not one but several attempts to normalize coinage and measures in her trading zones. A reduction in transactions costs would have more than repaid these efforts.

As Polanyi recognized, the large-scale inward movement of grain posed grave threats to Athenian society and values, since that flow was handled by metics and foreigners and brought the Athenian people into contact with alien views and behaviours. Solving the problem of bringing the wheat to the portals of Athens created another problem: how to insulate domestic culture from contact with foreign trading agents, commercial and monetary standards of wealth and status, and other pernicious influences? Athenian trade was never national trade, not only because Athens was not a nation, but also because it was in the hands of non-citizens. Foreign trade involved at least two factors disdained by the citizens: work and commercial gain. It was appropriate to tax such behaviour, and their importance was admitted, but citizens did not engage in them. Austin and Vidal-Naquet remark:

> The corn was imported by traders *(emporoi)* and sold by retail dealers *(sitopolai);* they were both metics, but their relations with the city did not have the same basis. The retail dealers were subjected to strict supervision and in particular to legislation which prohibited them from buying more than a limited quantity of corn at a time.[21]

They go on to quote from Lysias' *Tract Against the Corn Dealers*, directed at jurors who are asked to impose the death penalty for economic crimes.

The institutional theory conjectures that exchange grows most rapidly as trading arrangements are regularized and widely adopted. There is insufficient evidence to demonstrate that trade grew unusually quickly in the period between formation of the League and the Peloponnesian War, but it is a common impression and a useful hypothesis to put forward. The war left Athens weakened and unable to restore her empire. However, the continued strength of her navy and the further spread of her standard monetary instruments, weights and measures, and contract and maritime law contributed to another era of robust commerce. Polanyi goes so far as to say that an integrated grain market came into play during the late fourth century, which would be consistent with weakened political and cultural authority on the one hand, and the establishment of a uniform legal and commercial framework on the other, in which autochthonous agents could operate in an atmosphere of less overt State involvement.

### Free Riding and the Delian League

In examining the grain trade in the context of Athenian imperial relations, one finds a curious absence of force in its establishment and continuation. This is true both in the fifth century when Athens took advantage of the Persian retreat to assume leadership of the Delian League, and in the fourth century when, following the losses of the Peloponnesian War, the empire was reconstructed through Statecraft and negotiation. One explanation has already been put forth: the use of cultural bonds as a basis for legitimizing tributary demands and for the common institutional framework needed for the grain trade. An implication is that there were widely shared benefits of participating in the League's understandings, even if costs appear high to the modern observer. Since there were many cities scattered over a large area, it is hard to see immediately how Athens imposed its influence and why cities did not opt out of the system to avoid the payment of tribute. There seems to be a free-rider problem in that a city could enjoy the benefits of pirate-free waters and Athenian culture and commerce without paying dues.

Crude as it may have been, Athenian public finance was not immune to the difficulties that afflict any revenue system. Domestic liturgies and tax collections would have disintegrated without mechanisms for assigning responsibility and imposing harsh sanctions. Similarly, the imperial confederation would have collapsed if cities did not meet their obligations to provide ships, grain, and treasure. Although the alliance began voluntarily, Athenian leaders recognized almost immediately that it could not continue on this basis. Their aims show a parallel with those of a modern government or alliance: to collect revenues and keep the organization functioning, while fending off free-rider problems. The Athenians used force selectively. When Naxos tried to withdraw from the League, it was "besieged and crushed" by Athens, to use Finley's phrase.[22] The case is telling inasmuch as Athens' usual strategy was to eschew violence and coercion.

Making an example of one city's population was an excellent way of sending a message to other cities about Athens' resolve to keep the League intact. This illustrates the principle of "using maximum force in order to minimize the use of force." In modern public economic terms, what Athens did brilliantly was resolve the free-rider conundrum: the tendency of taxpayers not to meet their obligations to the collectivity while continuing to enjoy the benefits of public goods — in this case the protection of Athens and the League and a shared culture and economy that elevated life both socially and materially. In a similar vein, the Megarian Decree of Pericles in 432 excluded the Megarians, for their transgressions, from the Athenian orbit. His intent was to define the boundaries of the confederation and make it plain who was in and who was out, who would pay dues and enjoy the gains and who would not.

## Conclusion

A few simple principles will help guide us through an understanding of intersocial trade down through the ages. These account for the chief features of the Athenian grain trade, which was the material *sine qua non* of the imperial system and the classical age. In addition, new light has been shed on a few lingering puzzles, such as the tenacity with which Athens sought to extend the ambit of her laws and practices, especially the maritime codes and edicts affecting property and commerce, as well as the seemingly pointless effort to widen the use of her coinage and system of weights and measures.

The case of the Athenian grain trade is of more than idle historical interest. Analogies can be made with modern practices. There are elements of modern trading and payments networks that defy orthodox explanations resting on narrow definitions of self-interest and constricted resource- and factor-based determinisms on the supply side. A large volume of contemporary unrequited transfers follows kinship and cultural ties reminiscent of those that bound in spirit the ancient expatriate colonists to their Athenian heartland. In the Middle Ages, Europeans shifted large amounts of wealth to the Vatican. Non-resident south Asians living in the United States making deposits in banks on the subcontinent make little sense in conventional terms; an understanding of the motives for ancient Greek transfers could serve to illuminate this phenomenon.

Awareness of Athenian practices informs our comprehension of modern trade relations. Japan is not an economy driven by a witless need to export, as it is often perceived to be. Flooding the world with well-crafted products is hardly a reasonable policy aim in and of itself. The Japanese are merely subject to the same pressure that confronted the ancient Athenians: the need to import in order to survive and flourish as a civilization. Like Athens, Japan must import food, energy, and raw materials. The Japanese use of force proved futile; their imperial quest was thwarted by a congeries of superior powers, forcing them to rely on more subtle mechanisms. The Japanese first learned imperfectly, but then they mastered alien technological and commercial formulae. They increasingly integrated their economy into the world's exchange systems. Their apparent refutation of the supply-based laws of comparative cost stems from their recognition that the key to maximal participation in trade is organizational and institutional accommodation. Like the Athenians, too, they have been marvellously successful in insulating their economy and culture from penetration by alien agents bearing dissonant values and exhibiting unbecoming conduct.

**Notes**

1. Pearson 1977, xxx–xxxi.
2. For a fuller development of institutional theory, see Adams 1987.
3. Arnold 1957, 154.
4. Polanyi 1966, 99.
5. Polanyi 1966, 104.
6. These principles and their elaboration are taken with little change from Adams 1987.
7. Polanyi 1944.
8. A thorough history of demography and cultivation is Sallares 1991, who makes evident two points that are not adequately treated in my text. First, Attic agriculture was subject to a number of evolutionary trends involving yields, cropping patterns, and inputs; second, the total mix of agriculture encompassed a number of cereals, animals, and other products, such as grapes and olives, so that the sector was much more diverse than it seems, if one focuses primarily upon the production of and trade in grains. Moreover, the degree of dependence upon external supplies certainly varied from time to time, either on a trended basis or because of inclemencies.
9. A large portion of *The Livelihood of Man* is devoted to Athenian economic organization, within the city's political system, including the institutionalization of the grain trade. Polanyi stressed the two-fold character of that organization: the simultaneous and reinforcing expansion of both State controls and the market. What he called planning on an "unprecedented" scale was consistent with, even integral to, the equally "unprecedented" expansion of internal trade and the long-distance trade in provisions. See pp. 145ff.
10. Goldsmith 1987, 16–17. Everyone agrees that detailed accounts in modern form cannot be generated from the few numbers pertaining to economic transactions that have come down to us. The problem is not only the lapse of time and the loss of records, but that the Greeks had little or no interest in such matters. What is important is that the patterns Goldsmith outlines did obtain and that they are representative of the best scholarship on the subject. Also see Meiggs 1972, chapter 14 and appendix 12 on tributary flows.
11. Goldsmith 1987, 22.

12. Goldsmith 1987, 32.
13. Polanyi examined various estimates and numerical fragments in making his arguments. See Polanyi 1977, 200ff.
14. Goldsmith 1987, 29–30.
15. Meiggs 1972, 207. The titular classifications used in this paragraph are by no means unambiguous nor are the functions of the classes of officials named completely separable or understood.
16. Starr 1989, 40–41.
17. Cohen 1973.
18. Austin and Vidal-Naquet 1977, 116.
19. Austin and Vidal-Naquet 1977, 124–25.
20. Austin and Vidal-Naquet 1977, 326–27.
21. Austin and Vidal-Naquet 1977, 294–95.
22. Finley 1983, 43.

## References

Adams, John. 1987. "Trade and Payments as Instituted Process: The Institutional Theory of the External Sector." *Journal of Economic Issues* 21:1839–60. Reprinted in *Evolutionary Economics*. Vol. 2, *Institutional Theory and Policy*, edited by Marc. R. Tool, 421–42. Armonk, NY: M. E. Sharpe, 1988.

Arnold, Rosemary. 1957. "A Port of Trade: Whydah on the Guinea Coast." In *Trade and Market in the Early Empires*, edited by Karl Polanyi, Conrad M. Arensberg, and Harry W. Pearson, 154–76. Glencoe IL: Free Press.

Austin, M. M., and P. Vidal-Naquet. 1977. *Economic and Social History of Ancient Greece: An Introduction*. Berkeley: University of California Press.

Cohen, Edward E. 1973. *Ancient Athenian Maritime Courts*. Princeton: Princeton University Press.

Finley, Moses I. 1983. *Economy and Society in Ancient Greece*, edited by Brent D. Shaw and Richard P. Saller. London: Penguin.

Goldsmith, Raymond W. 1987. *Premodern Financial Systems: A Historical Comparative Study*. Cambridge: Cambridge University Press.

Meiggs, Russell. 1972. *The Athenian Empire*. Oxford: Clarendon Press.

Pearson, Harry W. 1977. "Editor's Introduction." In Polanyi 1977, xxv–xxxvi.

Polanyi, Karl. 1944. *The Great Transformation*. Holt Rinehart and Winston.

———. 1966. *Dahomey and the Slave Trade*. Seattle and London: University of Washington Press.

———. 1977. *The Livelihood of Man*, edited by Harry W. Pearson. New York: Academic Press.

Sallares, Robert. 1991. *The Ecology of the Ancient Greek World*. Ithaca, NY: Cornell University Press.

Starr, Chester G. 1989. *The Influence of Sea Power on Ancient History*. New York: Oxford University Press.

# 5

# Water Management as a Function of Locational and Appropriational Movements and the Case of the Classic Maya of Tikal*

Vernon L. Scarborough

The role of critical material resources in the evolution of social complexity has preoccupied anthropologists and historians for decades. Karl Polanyi's examinations of economic processes have strongly influenced anthropological concepts of the distribution and exchange of material resources. Trade and exchange in critical resources continue to be postulated as significant stimuli for complexity within and between communities. Nevertheless, there are other views of social complexity based on material resources, some emphasizing the protection or acquisition of material resources by force and championing the argument that warfare triggers greater social and political control. A recurrent hypothesis for the origins of civilization and political complexity is population pressure, since population crowding, too, is a direct function of the availability of critical resources. All of these positions, as well as combinations of them, continue to be used to explain social complexity. Although Polanyi's influence has been felt primarily in the overwrought formalist-substantivist debate, it is his comparative, cross-cultural insights concerning how and why critical material resources are organized (locational vs. appropriational movements — see below) through time and space that will be the focus of this paper.

A critical resource that has been isolated as a principal variable in the development of complex society is water.[1] Unlike other economic and political explanations for social complexity, the hydraulic hypothesis directly examines the influence of a unique

105

variable — this single most critical of human resources. It is the universal demand for water and its lack of ready availability in most complex societies that make it an extremely attractive resource for evaluating economic organization cross-culturally.

### Background

Water management involves the interruption and redirection of the natural movement or collection of water by society. Wittfogel[2] and Steward[3] championed a determinist role for water management in early States. This resulted in a series of debates as to the significance of the hydraulic hypothesis in the formation of stratified society.[4] An emphasis on political transformations and the sometimes strident tone of Wittfogel's work made for a comparatively strong reaction to his contribution.

As a student of Max Weber, Wittfogel emphasized the bureaucratic organization apparent in State formation. Agreeing with Marx's notions of an Asiatic mode of production, Wittfogel argued that, tied to an irrigation scheme, the early Chinese State promoted despotic control by expanding the division of labour to all levels of society. The bureaucracy did not require private property or individual notions of ownership; rather, it was based on what Giddens would call "possession," or the privilege of use.[5]

In Wittfogel's classic *Oriental Despotism: A Comparative Study of Total Power*, published in 1957 and immediately heralded as a landmark in political economy, he argued that hydraulic society was synonymous with Oriental despotism. If a society was more economically complex than that of simple subsistence agriculture, outside the influence of successful rainfall agriculture, and not based on a property-ownership industrial model, then hydraulic society could develop. Either water was relocated at great effort by mass labour allotment, or not at all.

This model for the origin of the State was promoted for each of the primary loci of early State development in the Old World and later generalized to the Western hemisphere.[6] Although Wittfogel's thesis has been severely criticized for its determinism, it does demonstrate a well-defined role for irrigation and significant landscape modification in semi-arid seats of early State formation. The hydraulic hypothesis cannot be viewed as the primary trigger in the origins or development of complex societies. But the theory did represent, within the disciplines of political anthropology and political economy, the first material-based explanation for the processes promoting State formation that was grounded on rigorous archaeological verification. The structure of Wittfogel's arguments allowed anthropologists and subsequent archaeologists to counter his primary trigger mechanism and pose other stimuli assailable from the archaeological record — trade, warfare, and resource symbiosis, eventually leading to the incorporation of population pressure models. The popularity of these latter perspectives, together with a recent resurgence in actor-based and ideologically directed interpretations for the beginnings of civilization, has led to a near dismissal of the importance of early water systems and the significance of the engineered landscape. Before reintroducing water management as an economic concern, the physical properties of water and its management will be briefly examined.

### Physical Characteristics of Water and its Management

The two characteristics of water that have most influenced early villages, towns, and cities are fluidity and gravity flow. Fluidity permits a liquid's ease of transport. Water does not usually require beasts of burden or wheeled vehicles for its immediate relocation, and thus its cost to the consumer tends to be intrinsically low. Gravity flow is the characteristic movement of a fluid from higher to lower elevations via a path of least resistance. It is the cardinal principle in the manipulation of water within a canal scheme, but in rugged areas it is the primary obstacle to water control — especially collection.

The properties of fluidity and gravity flow are responsible for two additional conditions imposed by human managers. The first involves the many mechanical problems associated with lifting water vertically. Its bulk and unwieldiness require sealed containers for this movement. The second condition is the ability to divert or abruptly cut the supply of water to a consumer. Diversion dams and conventional reservoirs with sluice gates permit individuals or a small group of users to treat water as a commodity in negotiating with other users. Unlike many other commodities, water is frequently a single-source medium. The initial investment in controlling water, particularly apparent in irrigation schemes, is to localized points of distribution through sluice gates and related features.

Three principal landscaping techniques comprise most water manipulations among early States. Wells, reservoirs and dams, and canals represent major earth-moving investments demanding significant labour, exact timing, and precision in both construction and maintenance. Some societies appear to emphasize reservoir management, while others focus on canal distributary systems. The physical investments tend to be in either collection or diversion — source as opposed to allocation. Although considerable variability exists, this dichotomy is further defined in the cases of environments consisting of arid settings associated with navigable rivers and those identified as humid settings without navigable rivers. This dichotomy is a useful one for the earliest States, but it collapses with the spread of stratified society globally. Not surprisingly, the incidence of reservoir construction does appear to correlate with the absence of perennial drainages, while canal systems are associated with more predictable riverine allotments.

Much has been written about canal systems and other techniques used to relocate water and the labour force necessary to construct and maintain an adequate water supply. Although sizeable natural watersheds provide permanent and more or less predictable quantities of water, shortages can be induced by human agency. Nevertheless, seasonal fluctuations are well understood and water requirements can be scheduled accordingly. Attention in these systems has been directed to allocation decisions. Based on an irrigation model, they involve the size of the area to be watered, the amount and timing of the release, and the established rules and traditional formulas affecting distribution.

Little scholarly attention has been paid to those sources that are almost completely constructed by humans. Although allocation decisions remain important in such systems, other factors weigh heavily. Where water collection is a deliberate action requiring construction and maintenance of special fixtures, a different set of organizational principles is implied. In some areas of the world, entire watersheds were created to accommodate the water demands of a thriving community. The classic-period Maya Lowlands provide a case in point. The adaptations made by the ancient Sinhalese are another. These two examples also differ in important respects. The karstic conditions of the Maya Lowlands — and the elevated seepage rates implied — made site paving absolutely necessary, while the Sinhalese of northern Sri Lanka adapted to the paucity of water by damming small rivers behind huge collection tanks.

Unlike canal distributary systems that assume the overall availability of water from a faraway and sizeable watershed, reservoir/catchment area systems demand immediate and persistent attention to their watersheds. The physical positioning of goods and people over the landscape in this adaptation is expectedly different from that associated with a canalized system.

Another variety of "still-water" management is the modification of lake margins and internally drained, seasonally inundated wetlands. These systems assume the source's initial availability, but can entail sizeable reclamation projects with investment in raised or drained fields. Acceptable water levels and degrees of purity depend on landscape engineering. How water is stored in the still-water channels between fields is critical. Too much water and the fields are flooded, too little water and plant desiccation results. Further, accelerated sedimentation rates and/or uncontrolled mineralization are as much a concern to still-water managers as to irrigation managers.

Storage is the problem that drives reservoir organization as well as other still-water adaptations. The seasonal variation in the availability of water, and its sometimes erratic arrival even during the rainy season, makes the physical preparation and maintenance of the rainfall runoff catchment area critical for establishing sufficient quantities of water in storage.

### Economic Aspects of Water Management

Halperin[7] has recently reintroduced Polanyi's concept of the "economy as instituted process."[8] She suggests that a formal model for the economy should include more than just a category for "locational movements," or the physical changes induced by humans in the material stuffs of livelihood and/or the relocation of goods or people from one area to another. Her analysis indicates that ecological studies have emphasized locational movements but have devoted less attention to the principles underlying human organization and factors relating to the transfer of rights, or "appropriational movements." Halperin writes:

> Appropriational movements ... consist of: (1) *organizational changes*, or (2) *transfers of rights* .... Transfers of rights change people's access to and control over goods and resources. The ability to control goods and resources used in the production of surpluses to maintain large populations and the ability to acquire goods for simple and

direct consumption by producers are both examples of appropriational movements.[9]

The organization of labour associated with the construction and maintenance of a watershed source differs from that of a purely distributary system. Where the watershed of a community is its residential locus, a community-wide investment in watershed maintenance is required from a wide variety of spatially separated areas — unlike the maintenance organization associated with a ditch master's obligations with respect to fixed points along narrowly defined canal lengths. The water draining towards a human-modified catchment area and the associated reservoirs built to receive that water are not accessible or divisible until the source is canalized. Source systems emphasize community-wide activity, while allocation systems are more readily exploited by the special interests of an individual or a group.

How might the physical disposition of people and things over a landscape influence the organization of labour and resources? The task demands of maintenance on a reservoir system are legion. Although certain times of the year are more demanding in respect to monitoring flows and generating water stores, focused maintenance of the catchment must emphasize seepage-proof surfaces and waste debris removal even during the dry season. Heavy rainfall calls for a period of community co-ordination to make sure that runoff is directed to reservoirs and that the scouring action of moving water is minimized. In the somewhat exaggerated case of the southern Lowland Maya, the entire site was the catchment surface, with each household having a direct and immediate link to the quality of water.

Both locational and appropriational movements are fundamentally different in the reservoir/catchment area system as opposed to canal/distributary systems. It is posited that people did not relocate great distances to plant, maintain, or harvest their agricultural plots in the still-water model. Although reservoirs reached sizeable proportions, they were distinctly finite in capacity. The farther a household plot was from a reservoir source, the greater the likelihood that neighbouring households would exhaust the water supply. The adaptation was one to the immediate margins of the reservoir; the larger the capacity of the reservoir in a system, the larger the population in proximity.

Canal distributary organization encouraged field plots at almost any distance from the source, given the comparative abundance of a perennial riverine environment. When positioned on a plain, ancient cities were frequently horizontally gridded or radially planned with a set of field systems following the riverine course as far as transportation networks would accommodate. Communities compacted themselves at periodic intervals within the riverine system and still maintained their field plots some distance away. Because of the potential distances between communities and field plots, the agriculturalists operated in a more independent manner than did those who used a reservoir system. As Wittfogel argued, a bureaucracy was necessary in a canal distributary system to control land and water allotments and to prevent abuses.

These two arrangements (reservoir/catchment and canal/distributary) existed in the earliest States. It can be presumed that the immediate economic organization within a community dependent on catchment runoff reservoirs demanded a form of integration different from and more focused than that defined by outfield canalized plots. Given the volume of literature examining canal systems, perhaps a closer view of a reservoir-dependent water system from the southern Maya Lowlands is appropriate.

Many of the largest and best understood cities of the Maya area such as Tikal[10] and Caracol[11] are located in northeastern Petén, Guatemala, and northwestern Belize. This portion of the southern Maya Lowlands is considered the core zone of classic-period activity (A.D. 250-900), containing the highest density of people and the

## Figure 1
### Schematic Cross-section of a Classic Period Lowland Maya Microwatershed

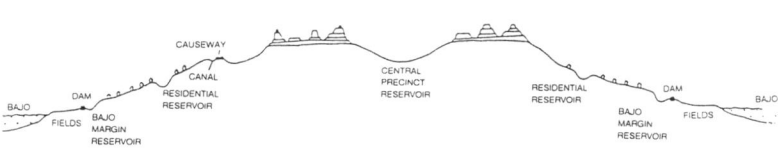

greatest investment in monumental architecture.[12] It is also an area of water deficiency. Although an annual precipitation rate of 2,000 mm is responsible for its semitropical vegetation, only 10 percent of this total comes during a four-month dry season.[13] Further, there are no springs or permanent streams of consequence.

In the Maya Lowlands, hillocks and promontories were modified through cut-and-fill quarry and construction activity to produce human-made micro-watersheds, inclusive of large elevated reservoirs (Figure 1).[14] Although the central precinct of an ancient Maya city was not a vacant ceremonial centre, residential occupation was more dense immediately outside the towering monumental architecture and sizeable plazas and courtyards of the hillock's summit. Reducing the amount of household trash that entered a reservoir system from the summit catchment area influenced the kind of dispersed settlement associated with Maya cities. At Tikal, for instance, little domestic midden debris exists near central-precinct buildings.[15] In a gravity-driven reconstruction, water was used initially for residential consumption and subsequently recycled into low-lying tanks in proximity to swamp-margin fields. At Tikal, again, approximately 9,800 people occupied the city's core, their water needs met by the main summit catchment area and reservoir system, which swelled to capacity in the wet season and was drained deliberately in the dry season. The reservoir system here as at several other landlocked southern Lowland cities was the sole source for water, the most critical of resources.

The sculpting of the engineered landscape resulted in a broadly paved catchment area canted and banked so as to direct precipitation into tanks and basins. Surplus water gained in this manner was not at all superfluous. Water shortfalls could have disastrous consequences. With increases in population, pavements were extended and reservoirs expanded. Although other factors precipitated the building activity associated with a Maya city, the quarry scars produced in constructing the pyramids, and the pavements used to surface the plazas and flanking structures, represent the reservoirs and catchment surfaces necessary for adequate water stores.

The preparation of the central-precinct surfaces required careful planning, with the emphasis on gradient relationships rather than horizontal grid or radial models of town planning. The perceived "randomness" sometimes associated with Maya settlement patterns may be a consequence of a Western bias toward urban planning and an inability to appreciate the verticality associated with settlement and water management. In the southern Maya Lowlands, the classic-period city of Tikal is perhaps the best example of this adaptation. Herein lies one definition of water organization for the Maya area.

### Tikal

Large well-defined reservoirs were identified early in the first mapping operations at Tikal (Figure 2).[16] The Maya of Tikal built a sophisticated human-made watershed designed to capture rainfall from the thick, impervious plastered surfaces covering the grand architecture and expansive plazas. Drawing on more than a thousand years of landscape modification, these Maya sculpted the limestone hills to allow gravity to drive the core community's water stores.[17]

## Figure 2
## Map of Tikal Catchment Areas and Reservoirs

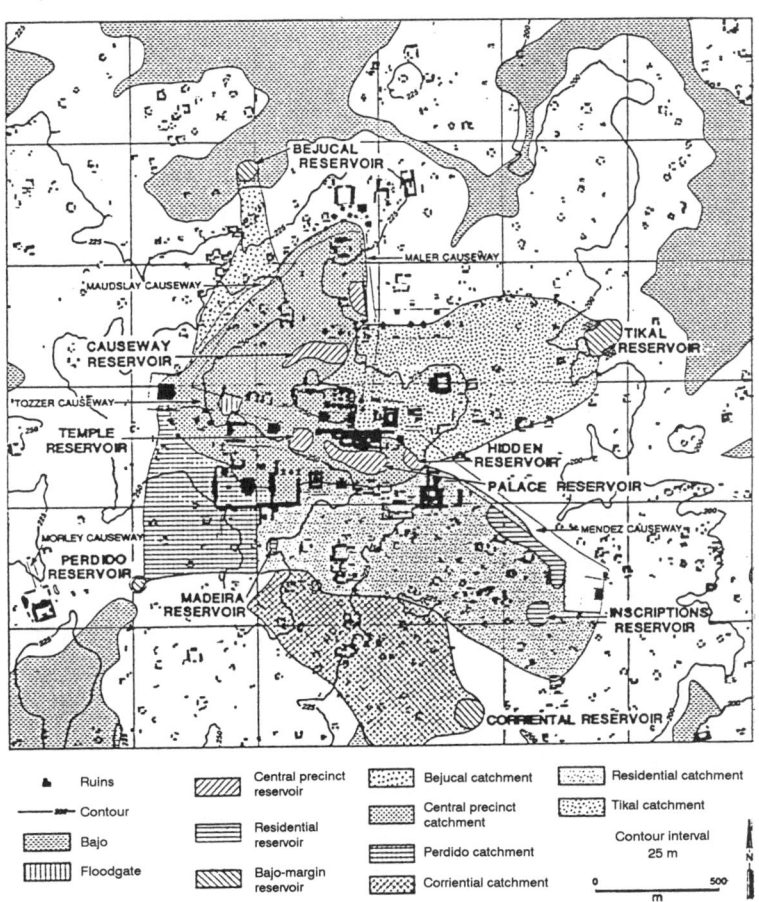

Tikal is defined by three reservoir types. Of the large tanks, the most numerous (six) are positioned near the summit of the city within the core or epicentre of the site. Dubbed central-precinct reservoirs, these basins had a combined capacity of between 100,000 and 240,000 cubic metres — each with a volume great enough to cover a football field several metres deep in water. Most of these features were dammed directly or indirectly by elevated causeways linking various portions of central Tikal. Controlled release of water from elevated reservoirs to downslope flanks and adjacent swamp margins would have provided potable water as well as moisture for crops during the dry season. Immediately below the summit within the most dense occupation at the site lie the residential reservoirs. These depressions are smaller than the other reservoir types identified.

At the foot of the ridge on which central Tikal rests are four large reservoirs positioned approximately equidistant from each other and located roughly in the cardinal directions from the epicentre of Tikal. These reservoirs have been identified as swamp-margin reservoirs because of their proximity to the swamps flanking the site (Figure 3). Including some of the largest reservoirs at Tikal, their combined volumes range between 50,000 and 170,000 cubic metres. They are positioned away from the largest concentrations of housemounds in central Tikal and are directly connected in at least two cases to the elevated central-precinct reservoirs by drainage channels. Their location may suggest an agricultural function, given the sophisticated manipulation of wetland settings by the Maya elsewhere.

The complexity of the Tikal water management system was not fully appreciated until the catchment areas feeding the reservoirs were analyzed. Six major catchment surfaces were identified, ranging from nine to sixty-two hectares (twenty-two to 153 acres). Water falling on these sloping surfaces was directed into the associated reservoirs in the central precinct of Tikal or directly into the low-lying swamp-margin reservoirs ultimately leading into the neighbouring

## Figure 3
### Map of Causeways and Reservoirs at Tikal

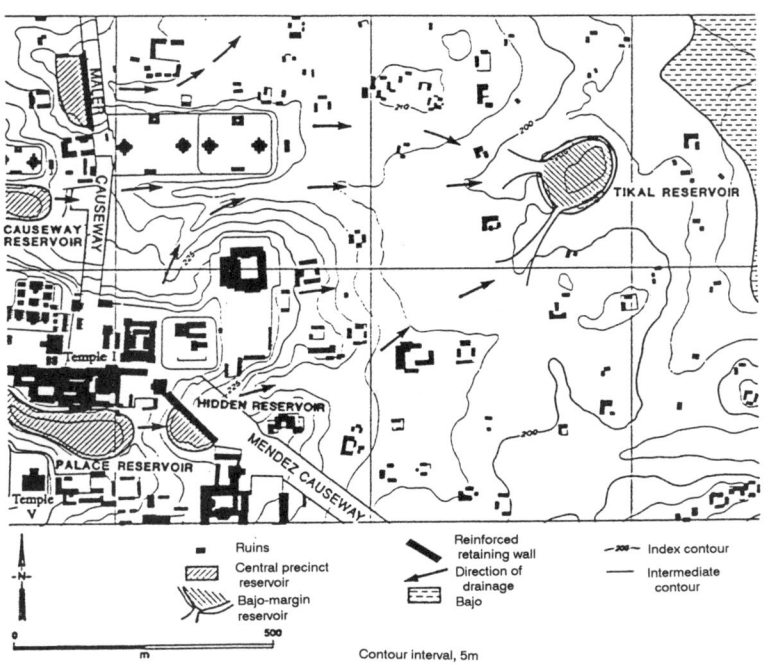

## Figure 4
### Reservoir and Catchment Dimensions at Tikal

| Reservoir type | No. | Reservoir capacity (m³) | Catchment area (ha) | Rainfall (m³/year) |
|---|---|---|---|---|
| Central precinct | 6 | 105,108–243,711 | 61.90 | 928,500 |
| Residential | 3 | 42,647–133,921 | 56.37 | 603,324 |
| *Bajo*-margin | 4 | 48,956–172,149 | 125.63 | 1,379,322 |
| *Pozas* | 47 | 8,581–12,867 | 37.96 | 379,508 |
| *Aguada*, other | 15 | 1,450–4,956 | 16.71 | 174,974 |

swamps. Drawing from monthly rainfall and evapotranspiration rates, coupled with seepage data taken from what is known about the individual catchments, estimates were made as to the amount of water entering the various reservoirs (Figure 4). The water management system was designed to accommodate the seasonal availability of the rainfall, the absence of permanent streams or springs, and the gentle topographical relief of the region. By using a gravity flow system, the ancient Maya were able to provide residential populations within and near the central precinct frequently replenished water stores during the dry season.

## Conclusion

As suggested elsewhere, reservoir-dependency centralized the water resource and may have influenced the political organization of the Maya.[18] Nevertheless, the Maya did not nucleate into large urban aggregates like some other early States based on canal distributary systems. The appropriational movements associated with water systems that emphasize watershed construction and maintenance may entail a less routinized scheduling of labour due to the less precise knowledge of when and how much actual rain will fall on a human-made watershed, and may generate a tendency to settle the landscape in a dispersed manner to maintain and deploy a labour force over a spatially wide water catchment area, the settlement being partially determined by the natural contours of the watershed. Although factors other than water clearly influenced the locational and appropriational movements of the Maya economy, watershed maintenance was a significant organizing principle — less apparent in many riverine-based, canal-dependent States.

The concepts of locational and appropriational movements permit a useful approach for assessing the economic organization of ancient water systems. Locational movements illustrate the physical dichotomy between water systems that emphasize source or watershed dependency as opposed to distribution- or canal-oriented systems. Appropriational movements offer a window through which to glimpse how communities dependent on rain-water catchment and reservoir systems might organize their labour force differently from those that feature the canal-based system. In a complex society, the tendency to organize spatially within centralized, compacted — many times nucleated — communities appears to have been offset by dispersed settlement patterns when the uncertainty of fluctuating and seasonal rainfall required a different economic organization. At Tikal and other ancient Maya cities, we see many factors other than market convenience affecting economic organization. This would hardly have surprised Polanyi, but what is especially remarkable in these cases is the primary role played by social institutions for water management in the economic process.

## Notes

1. Wittfogel 1957; Scarborough 1991a.
2. Wittfogel 1957; 1972.
3. Steward 1949; 1955.
4. Leach 1959; Millon 1962; Mitchell 1973; Service 1975; Hunt and Hunt 1976; Scarborough 1991b.
5. Giddens 1971, 26.
6. Wittfogel 1972.
7. Halperin 1988; 1989.
8. Polanyi 1957.
9. Halperin 1989, 18.
10. Coe 1965; 1967; Coe and Haviland 1982.
11. Beetz and Satterthwaite 1981; Chase and Chase 1987.
12. Culbert and Rice 1990.
13. Scarborough and Gallopin 1991.
14. Scarborough 1993; Scarborough, Connolly, and Ross 1993.
15. Harrison 1993.
16. Carr and Hazard 1961.
17. Scarborough and Gallopin 1991.
18. Scarborough and Gallopin 1991.

## References

Beetz, Carl P., and Linton Satterthwaite. 1981. *The Monuments and Inscriptions of Caracol, Belize*. Philadelphia: University of Pennsylvania Press.
Carr, Robert F., and James E. Hazard. 1961. *Map of the Ruins of Tikal, El Petén, Guatemala*. Tikal Report no. 11. Philadelphia: University of Pennsylvania Press.
Chase, Arlen F., and Diane Z. Chase. 1987. *Investigations at the Classic Maya City of Caracol, Belize: 1985–1987*. San Francisco: Pre-Columbian Art Research Institute, Monograph 3.
Coe, William R. 1965. "Tikal, Guatemala and Emergent Maya civilization." *Science* 147:1401–19.
———. 1967. *Tikal: A Handbook of the Ancient Maya Ruins*. Philadelphia: University of Pennsylvania Press.
Coe, William R., and William A. Haviland. 1982. *Introduction to the Archaeology of Tikal, Guatemala*. Tikal Report no. 12. Philadelphia: University of Pennsylvania Press.
Culbert, T. Patrick, and Don S. Rice, eds. 1990. *Precolumbian Population History in the Maya Lowlands*. Albuquerque: University of New Mexico Press.
Giddens, Anthony. 1971. *Capitalism and Modern Social Theory*. Cambridge: Cambridge University.
Halperin, Rhoda H. 1988. *Economies across Cultures*. London: Macmillan.
———. 1989. "Ecological versus Economic Anthropology: Changing 'Place' vs. Changing 'Hands'." *Research in Economic Anthropology* 11:15–41.
Harrison, Peter D. 1993. "Aspects of Water Management in the Southern Maya Lowlands." In *Economic Aspects of Water Management in the Prehispanic New World*, edited by Vernon L. Scarborough and Barry L. Isaac. *Research in Economic Anthropology*, Supplement 7. Greenwich, CT: JAI Press.
Hunt, Robert C., and Eva Hunt. 1976. "Canal Irrigation and Local Social Organization." *Current Anthropology* 17:389–411.
Leach, Edmund R. 1957. "Hydraulic Society in Ceylon." *Past and Present* 15:2–26.
Millon, Rene. 1962. "Variation in Social Responses to the Practice of Irrigation Agriculture." In *Civilization in Arid Lands*, edited by R. B. Woodbury, 56–88. Salt Lake City: University of Utah Anthropological Papers, Number 62.
Mitchell, William P. 1973. "The Hydraulic Hypothesis: A Reappraisal." *Current Anthropology* 14:532–34.
Polanyi, Karl. 1957. "The Economy as Instituted Process." In *Trade and Market in the Early Empires*, edited by Karl Polanyi, Conrad M. Arensberg, and Harry W. Pearson, 243–69. Glencoe, IL: Free Press.
Scarborough, Vernon L. 1991a. "Water Management Adaptations in Non-Industrial Complex Societies: An Archaeological Perspective." In *Archaeological Method and Theory*, Volume 3, edited by Michael B. Schiffer, 101–54. Tucson: University of Arizona Press.
———. 1991b. Review of *Canal Irrigation in Prehispanic Mexico: The Sequence of Technological Change*, by William E. Doolittle (Austin: University of Texas Press, 1990). *Journal of Field Archaeology* 8:518–20.

———. 1993. "Water Management in the Southern Maya Lowlands: An Accretional Model for the Engineered Landscape." In *Economic Aspects of Water Management in the Prehispanic New World*, edited by Vernon L. Scarborough and Barry L. Isaac. *Research in Economic Anthropology*, Supplement 7. Greenwich, CT: JAI Press.

Scarborough, Vernon L., Robert P. Connolly, and Steven P. Ross. 1993. "The Prehispanic Maya Reservoir System at Kinal, Petén, Guatemala." *Ancient Mesoamerica* 4:forthcoming.

Scarborough, Vernon L., and Garry G. Gallopin. 1991. "A Water Storage Adaptation in the Maya Lowlands." *Science* 251:658–62.

Service, Elman R. 1975. *Origins of the State and Civilization: The Process of Cultural Evolution*. New York: W. W. Norton.

Steward, Julian H. 1949. "Cultural Causality and Law: A Trial Formation of the Development of Early Civilizations." *American Anthropologist* 51:1–27.

———, ed. 1955. *Irrigation Civilizations: A Comparative Study*. Washington: Pan-American Union.

Wittfogel, Karl A. 1957. *Oriental Despotism: A Comparative Study of Total Power*. New Haven: Yale University Press.

———. 1972. "The Hydraulic Approach to Pre-Spanish Mesoamerica." In *Chronology and Irrigation: The Prehistory of the Tehuacan Valley*, Volume 4, edited by Frederick Johnson, 59–80. Austin: University of Texas.

# 6

# *Hansatsu:* Local Currencies in Pre-Industrial Japan*

## Makoto Maruyama

In many ways, Karl Polanyi broke new ground in his studies on what he called the semantics of money-uses. The general message is that the ways in which monies are used are manifold and above all determined by social context. In a generalized market economy, for example, monies usually appear as multi-purpose monies. By contrast, they usually appear as special-purpose monies in non-market economies, that is, economies not dominated by the self-regulating market system. Monies in non-market societies can also be categorized according to the distinction between internal and external money.[1] Polanyi studied the functioning of monies as it related to ancient Athens, but he never developed the theme in print.[2] Although I cannot therefore draw directly on Polanyi's work here, I believe that my approach is in keeping with Polanyi's spirit and aims and that it is important to try to shed light on the institutional separation between internal money and external money in the case of pre-industrial Japan.

Tokugawa Japan, which lasted between 1600 and 1868, had a unique monetary system. On the one hand, there was a group of metal monies which circulated in most parts of the country. On the other hand, a considerable number of local fiefs had their own paper

---

\* *The first version of this paper was presented at the Fourth International Karl Polanyi Conference, held in Montréal in November 1992. I would like to thank the editors for useful comments that have increased the clarity of my discussion.*

currencies. Prior to the Tokugawa era, there had been metal monies of different origins. Among these, copper coins imported from China were the most common currencies for ordinary market transactions. There were also gold and silver ingots which were minted by local lords in the fifteenth and sixteenth centuries. These ingots were used in relatively large-scale market transactions. In addition to these, there were special kinds of monies used by Hideyoshi Toyotomi, the Shogun prior to Ieyasu Tokugawa in the late 1580s. Hideyoshi minted elliptical gold coins called *oban* and *koban*. These gold coins were mainly used not for market transactions, but for gift-giving and for military purposes.

When the Tokugawa family achieved hegemony over the other feudal powers at the beginning of the seventeenth century, the family started monopolizing the seigniorage through its direct control of major mines. Since the gold monies were less popular than the silver ingots, the unification of the minting of gold monies was easier than that of silver ingots. Ieyasu Tokugawa, the first Tokugawa Shogun, called in Hideyoshi's *oban* and *koban* and put new coins in circulation. By the end of the 1660s, the unification of the minting of gold monies was completed. By contrast, since silver ingots were widely used in market transactions in various areas, especially in the western part of Japan, it took several more decades for the government to replace the local silver ingots with Tokugawa's own silver ingots.

The Tokugawa government started minting copper coins in 1636. In contrast to the gold and silver monies, the government minted copper coins in order to meet the increasing demand for lower-value coins coming from the markets. The old copper coins were banned in 1670, when the government had concluded that the supply of new copper coins was meeting the demand.

The gold, silver and copper monies of Tokugawa Japan were all designed to serve as standard currencies throughout Japan. However, there were social and geographical differences in the people's choices of currencies. Feudal lords preferred gold money for their transactions in both market and non-market situations. Merchants used both gold and silver monies, but they usually preferred silver to gold, because the former could be used for both large- and small-scale transactions. Peasants and common people mostly used copper coins for purchasing basic goods and necessities.

From the geographical point of view, gold money was preferred in the Edo area (later called Tokyo) and in the rest of eastern Japan, whereas silver money was more commonly chosen in Osaka and in western Japan. Copper money was used all over Japan. The preference for gold money in eastern Japan was based on the preponderance of more feudal economic forms in Edo, whereas the preference for silver money in western Japan was due to the higher development of commerce in Osaka. The ubiquity of the use of copper money stemmed from its very nature as a convenient common currency for small-scale, local market transactions.

The use of paper money as another local currency had been started by the merchants in the Ise area in central Japan in the sixteenth century. The merchants aimed at substituting paper money for silver money. Ise was one of the holy places of Shintoism, and was governed by a regional authority that was relatively independent from the feudal powers. In accordance with the growth of the commercial cities in the Ise area, the demand for currencies in the cities increased. The merchants in Ise, who had used commercial bills among themselves as early as the fifteenth century, gradually extended the use of commercial bills to the sphere of ordinary market transactions, and used them as a means of exchange. The commercial bills in the Ise area thus became a kind of private currency, whose credibility was ensured by the reserves of metal money held by the merchants. In the same way as in Ise, the use of private paper money was introduced in other cities in the central part of Japan.

However, the Tokugawa unification of the coinage was extended also to these private paper monies. In the 1620s and 1630s, the government restricted the issue of private paper to the Ise area, allowing it there only because of its special religious role.

Up to the middle of the seventeenth century, the money supply as regulated by the Tokugawa government seemed to be meeting the demand for currencies in markets. However, such a monopolized supply of money had its own functional limits. Firstly, no commodities had national markets. Although there were large markets in the large cities, which were regulated by the Tokugawa government, these markets remained as relatively independent meeting places for traders. Beside these markets there was a vast number of castle-town markets and village-town markets. These local markets were usually regulated by the local fief authorities, rather than by the Tokugawa government. The markets in the large cities and the local markets were therefore institutionally discrete. This meant that the supply of money from the Tokugawa government in metropolitan markets did not always meet the demand for currencies in the local markets. Accordingly, there was always a tendency toward currency shortages in those local fiefs in which markets were growing. Secondly, the large number of fiefs ruled by the local clans, especially by the clans that had antagonized the Tokugawa family when the Tokugawa regime was established, suffered from a shortage of money from the very beginning of the Tokugawa era.

During the latter half of the seventeenth century, in order to solve these problems some of the local authorities started issuing still another kind of local paper currency, which is now called *hansatsu*, or feudal-clan note. There were two patterns for issuing *hansatsu*. The first involved direct issuing by the local authorities. An issuing section was set up within each local government, and the chief treasurer of the government also served as chief of the issuing section. He controlled the issuing of *hansatsu* and managed the metal-money reserve. The actual issuers were selected from among the chartered merchants, who came from the large cities or from within the same area. They supplied the reserve money for converting *han-*

*satsu*, and executed the issuing operation. The second pattern involved indirect issuing. In this case, the local authorities gave the right of issuing *hansatsu* to the chartered merchants instead of establishing an issuing section of their own. The chartered merchants, in return, laid their landed property in pledge and made appropriate payments to the local authorities.

Since any *hansatsu* was designed after the local paper currency, it was, in principle, convertible into metal monies. In practice, however, the local authorities usually forbade the conversion of *hansatsu* into metal monies for use within their territory. Therefore, the conversion of *hansatsu* into metal monies could happen only when people left a territory. By the same token, people had to convert their monies into *hansatsu* when they entered any particular local territory. In this manner, *hansatsu* became the local currency in various areas in Japan.

Although the Tokugawa government never granted seigniorage rights to local fiefs, it left the issuing of *hansatsu* to take its own course as long as *hansatsu* remained a local currency. In consequence, *hansatsu* served as internal money for the people in the feudal-clan territory, whereas metal money served as external money.

The first *hansatsu* was issued in 1661 in northern Japan in Fukui *han* (a feudal-clan territory is now called a *han*). The number of fiefs that had their own *hansatsu* steadily increased during the Tokugawa era.[3] In the seventeenth century, forty-three fiefs out of 257 (16 percent) had their own *hansatsu*. In the eighteenth century, the figure was doubled, and ninety fiefs out of 266 (34 percent) used *hansatsu*. In the nineteenth century, 139 fiefs out of 275 (50 percent) issued their own *hansatsu*.

The practice of issuing *hansatsu* spread faster in the western part of Japan than in the eastern. For example, in the Chugoku and Shikoku areas, in which commercial transactions developed widely around the Inland Sea of Seto, 38.5 percent of the fiefs were already issuing *hansatsu* in the seventeenth century. This percentage increased to 71.8 in the eighteenth century, to 88.1 in the nineteenth. By contrast, in the Tohoku area, which is in the northeastern, rice-cropping region, the percentage of *hansatsu*-issuing fiefs remained as low as 10 in the seventeenth and the eighteenth centuries, and increased to only 18.2 in the nineteenth century.

Generally speaking, larger fiefs started using *hansatsu* earlier than smaller fiefs. The size of a fief in the Tokugawa era was officially determined to be the equivalent of its annual rice production. The quantity of rice was calculated in *koku* (one *koku* equals 5.11 bushels). For example, the Tokugawa family, the largest feudal clan, had a fief of 7 million *koku*, and this meant that the annual production of the fief was 7 million *koku* of rice. In the seventeenth century, 50 percent of the fiefs larger than 100 thousand *koku* used *hansatsu*, whereas 9.1 percent of the fiefs smaller than 100 thousand *koku* issued *hansatsu*. In the eighteenth century, 63 percent of the larger fiefs issued *hansatsu*, whereas 27.7 percent of the smaller fiefs did. In the nineteenth century, these percentages reached 74 and 45.3.

The expansion of the use of *hansatsu* corresponded roughly with the growth of markets.[4] In the large cities, there were large markets for agricultural produce as well as craft products. These metropolitan markets functioned as centres for interregional trade, and also stimulated local markets. For example, in Osaka there were enormous markets for daily necessities. Processed foods, cotton goods, and oil were popular products produced and sold in Osaka. The raw materials for these products were brought in from the suburban areas of Osaka; the finished products were then sent out to those areas. In Kyoto, there were markets for traditional craft items, such as silk products and goldware. The raw materials for these products were imported from all over Japan. The products in Kyoto were often sent to Edo markets where lords and warriors needed them. Edo was a huge consumer city, and there were various markets there for daily necessities. Most of those products were imported from Osaka in the first half of the Tokugawa era. The markets in Edo therefore served as additional stimuli for commerce in the western part of Japan. In the second half of the Tokugawa era, Edo also acquired the function of trading centre for the eastern part of Japan, and the area around Edo came to supply necessities to this large city.

Overall, the trade between fiefs was thus mediated and expanded by the metropolitan markets throughout the Tokugawa era. In the second half of the Tokugawa era, however, trade between fiefs was also sometimes direct, bypassing the large cities. In this manner, interregional trade came to form a complex, nation-wide network.

It should be noted, however, that the markets in Tokugawa Japan exemplify one of Polanyi's main theoretical arguments, since they were primarily embedded within what he called a redistributive form of social integration. Among various types of markets, the rice market was the largest. Local lords collected rice from peasants as rent, and distributed it among their warriors. The lords and warriors then changed rice for money in the castle-town markets. The rice markets in castle-towns thereby contributed to the redistribution of rice among the warriors. The markets for agricultural produce and daily necessities were thus formed around the rice markets. In each fief, the interdependence of the castle-town and its villages was obvious. Peasants were the suppliers of food to the town, and sought those daily necessities which they themselves could not produce. The raw materials for manufacturing the daily necessities were also brought from the villages to the castle-town.

The trade between the castle-town and the villages was usually mediated by small village-towns. At the beginning, only a limited range of retail goods was allowed to be traded in village-towns. Peasants had to visit the castle-town to purchase goods which were not available in village-towns. As time went by, however, peasants started to sell their own products in the markets in village-towns, and some of them became petty merchants.

From a social point of view, and as students of Polanyi will be unsurprised to learn, the growth of these local markets in Tokugawa Japan did not automatically bring about a capitalistically organized market economy. Even when peasants were involved in market transactions, and this was often the case from the very beginning of the Tokugawa era, they made use of market transactions in order to sustain their farming activities. The following episode illustrates the typical relationship between peasants and markets.[5] It is reported that in 1842 a peasant in eastern Japan made a plea to the authorities to allow him to engage in money-earning side-businesses because he had become sick and could not otherwise sustain his household. The historians who report this episode rightly interpret the peasant's plea as an expression of a wish to continue rather than quit peasant farming.

The need for money in local markets was one of the serious issues for each fief. Since the Tokugawa government forced local lords to make compulsory visits to Edo and demanded other compulsory services from their families, the lords usually needed very large amounts of funds. They therefore not only sent their rice for Edo for consumption purposes, but also caused rice to be brought into Osaka markets to have it exchanged for money. Currency deficits of the local governments, which I mentioned earlier, often stemmed from this feudal mechanism, because monies in fiefs tended to go outside. The use of *hansatsu* compensated for this tendency. In turn, however, problems due to excess *hansatsu* tended to arise because the *han* authorities often resorted to the issuing of *hansatsu* in order to save funds for their expenditure.

Excessive issuing of *hansatsu* sometimes resulted in crises in the local markets. On such occasions, the *han* authorities executed a moratorium until the economy regained balance. The economic crises caused by the excessive issuing of *hansatsu* were often followed by protests and uprisings of the common people in cities and villages. Such disruptions occurred about every fifteen years in the seventeenth century, and every three years in the eighteenth and nineteenth centuries. Thus the expanded use of *hansatsu* corresponded also to the increased problems due to their very use.[6] The problems due to *hansatsu* were not, however, in all cases uncontrollable. While uprisings in villages became more frequent in the nineteenth century as compared to the eighteenth, uprisings in cities became less frequent. It is also clear that the uprisings in the larger fiefs took place very frequently in the eighteenth century, and then became rare in the nineteenth. By contrast, in the smaller fiefs, uprisings took place more often in the nineteenth century. These patterns suggest that those fiefs that started using *hansatsu* in the earlier stage accumulated more knowledge about their nature, and thus they succeeded better at controlling the quantity of the local currency.

Although some Japanese historians have characterized *hansatsu* as unstable money because its abuses often led to uprisings,[7] it should be noted that there were still a great many *han* that seldom experienced *hansatsu* uprisings. Even when such uprisings took place, they were often due to sudden changes in external conditions, such as a change in the monetary policy of the Tokugawa government, or price changes in Osaka markets.

The following example will illustrate the flexibility allowed by *hansatsu*, rather than its supposedly fragile character.[8] In Okayama *han*, situated near the Inland Sea of Seto in western Japan, the local authorities were concerned about keeping an adequate reserve for issuing *hansatsu*, and often called in excess *hansatsu* from circulation. The first *hansatsu* in Okayama *han* was issued in 1679. It was put into circulation either through allowing its exchange for metal money or through government spending. *Hansatsu* returned to the government either through conversion into metal monies or through tax collection in *hansatsu*. In the 1730s, Okayama *han* experienced a money shortage. The *han* government therefore decided to acquire reserve money from interregional trade. In 1731, the government set up an agency to monopolize the cotton trade, and earmarked the profit from it as reserve for *hansatsu*. Also, by calling in the excess *hansatsu* promptly, the *han* government succeeded in stabilizing the circulation of *hansatsu* for more than a hundred years.

The system collapsed in 1854. There were large-scale uprisings in and around the castle-town of Okayama which resulted in the suspension of the convertibility of *hansatsu* into metal monies. The crisis was triggered by the sudden change in the foreign policy of the Tokugawa government. In 1854, the Tokugawa government had to give up its autarky because Admiral Perry from the United States threatened to open the borders of Japan. The feudal framework of Tokugawa Japan had ceased to be sustainable. When the Tokugawa regime came to an end in 1868, a new government was established by royalists who intended to turn Japan into a Westernized nation-state. As part of their centralization policies, they started to replace *hansatsu* with national paper currency. As a result of this replacement, local currencies ceased to exist in Japan, and were buried in oblivion.

By way of conclusion it can be noted that the study of pre-industrial local currencies has contemporary relevance. Local currencies can serve as tools for sustaining and safeguarding human subsistence on local and regional social scales. If we aim to think seriously about the decommodification of money, we should look into the ample experience of the use of local currencies in human history. Even today, we find that certain types of local money are still preserved in some non-market societies, such as the stone money in the Yap Islands. We also find new experiments with the local-currency idea in industrial societies, such as the "green dollar" system on Vancouver Island in Canada. The experience with local money in pre-industrial Japan can help us to think that the re-embedding of monies in social contexts is not only feasible but also desirable.

## Notes

1. Heinrich Schurtz broke ground in the study of what he called *Binnengeld* and *Außengeld* in small-scale societies (Schurtz 1898, 6; 1900, 292–97).
2. Polanyi 1977, 258–72.
3. The following data are based on Tsuchiya and Yamaguchi 1974; 1975.
4. The following account of the growth of markets owes much to Hayami and Miyamoto 1988; Shimbo and Saito 1989.
5. Fukaya and Kawanabe 1988.
6. Aoki 1975.
7. Kokusho 1928.
8. Kawade 1991; Okayama-City 1966.

## References

Aoki, Koji. 1975. *Hyakusho ikki sogo nenpyo* [Chronological table of peasant uprisings]. Tokyo: San-ichi Shobo.
Fukaya, Katsumi, and Sadao Kawanabe. 1988. *Edo jidai no morokasegi* [Earnings in the Edo period]. Tokyo: No-san-gyoson Bunka Kyokai.
Hayami, Yu, and M. Miyamoto, eds. 1988. *Nihon keizai shi* [Japanese economic history], vol. 1. Tokyo: Iwanami Shoten.
Kawade, Tatsumi. 1991. *Okayama han ni okeru hansatsu no kenkyu* [A study of hansatsu in Okayama]. Tokyo: Institute of Financial Studies, Bank of Japan.
Kokusho, Iwao. 1928. *Hoken shakai no tosei to toso* [Controls and protests in feudal society]. Tokyo: Kaizosha.
Okayama-City. 1966. *Okayama shishi* [The history of Okayama-City]. Okayama: Okayama-City.
Polanyi, Karl. 1977. *The Livelihood of Man*, edited by Harry W. Pearson. New York: Academic Press.
Schurtz, Heinrich. 1898. *Grundriß einer Entstehungsgeschichte des Geldes*. Beiträge zur Volks- und Völkerkunde, Band 5. Weimar: Emil Felber.
———. 1900. *Urgeschichte der Kultur*. Leipzig: Bibliographisches Institut.
Shimbo, Hiroshi, and O. Saito, eds. 1989. *Nihon keizai shi* [Japanese economic history], vol. 2. Tokyo: Iwanami Shoten.
Tsuchiya, Takao, and K. Yamaguchi, eds. 1974. *Nihon no kahei* [Monies in Japan], vol. 5. Tokyo: Toyo-keizai Shimposha.
———, eds. 1975. *Nihon no kahei* [Monies in Japan], vol. 6. Tokyo: Toyo-keizai Shimposha.

# 7

## Potatoes, Muskets, and a Changing Community: Economic Roles of Women and Slaves in Maori Society, 1769-1839[*]

### William C. Schaniel

A commonly held view among historians and anthropologists of non-European peoples is that contact with Europeans and adoption of Western technologies both tend to disembed established modes of livelihood from their social contexts. European systems and technology are believed to displace traditional systems and technology, resulting in the destruction or collapse of the traditional society.[1] This virological approach to Western contact assumes that change engendered by Western ideas and materials inherently leads to the dissolution of traditional culture, or put simply, change leads to collapse. No distinctions are made among processes of change, implying that all changes are similar. Scholars writing about New Zealand and the Maori (the native New Zealand Polynesians) have employed this model in their analyses.[2] The general argument is that Western "ideas were destructive,"[3] resulted in the "collapse of traditional values and confidence,"[4] and left the "culture and economy largely destroyed."[5] This paper will argue that ideas developed by Karl Polanyi in *The Great Transformation*[6] provide an alternate framework to the virological theory for the interpretation and evaluation of

---

[*] *The author gratefully acknowledges the advice, comments, and encouragement of Walter C. Neale, and also thanks Anne Mayhew for her continued support and Liz Key for her editorial assistance. The author dedicates this paper to the memory of Benjamin D. Joyner, Jr. The first version of this paper was read at the fourth International Polanyi Conference, held in Montréal in November 1992.*

such change. This framework will be applied to the economic history of the Maori prior to colonization, with some surprising results. Two European innovations — firearms and the cultivation of white potatoes — changed the roles of women, slaves and men. These changing roles changed the substance of Maori community life in surprising ways, but left modes of livelihood embedded.

**Polanyi and Change**

The ideas developed by Karl Polanyi in his published works provide a framework for interpreting recurring processes within economic systems and also for evaluating patterns of change. Polanyi's three forms of integration — reciprocity, redistribution, and market — provide a framework within which patterns of economic systems can be analyzed. The interpretive framework for classifying fundamental change is the process of what he called disembedding.

Polanyi's approach to economic analysis starts from the quasi-ethical proposition "that man's economy, as a rule, is submerged in his social relationships."[7] This concept of economic activity being more or less submerged within the general social order is critical to interpreting the consequences of different patterns of economic integration. First, the categories, divisions and associations of European ethics are not necessarily appropriate for the analysis of non-European societies. The appropriateness of groupings, divisions and connections of activities depends upon the valuing system(s) of a society. Second, changes in the patterns of economic integration necessarily require the disembedding of institutions, and the re-embedding or establishment of a separate ethical system. This complex analytical perspective is an important theme in *The Great Transformation*.

The dominant concern of *The Great Transformation* was the change in livelihood to a self-regulating market system. This transition involved the disembedding of economic institutions from other institutions.[8] The disembedding resulted from a restructuring of the rules of access to land, labour and money so that they would be subject to commodity rules — that is, considered under the rubric of price alone. With respect to property law, the various rights associated with what Polanyi called the fictitious commodities had to be separated and rebundled in accordance with a more individualistic conception of property.

Traditional property-rights theory separates property rights into three categories: 1) use rights, the right to access property; 2) usufruct rights, the right to claim the fruits or bounty of property; and 3) alienation rights, the right to transfer control of property permanently. The process of disembedding discussed in *The Great Transformation* was a process of reorganizing property rights. In a self-regulating market system, the property rights are all individual property rights — that is, all three kinds of rights are controlled by the same individual or group. Prior to the rise of the self-regulating market system, property rights were divided among and thus controlled by several groups. In *The Great Transformation* the enclosure movement simultaneously separated the peasants from their historic use and usufruct rights in the commons and bundled together all property rights under the control of the manor's lord. The separation of land and labour and the reorganization of property rights were necessary for the rise of a self-regulating market system. It was necessary that all commodities, whether final products or resources, be acquirable only by reference to price. Thus, the rules governing economic behaviour were changed and separated from the rules governing other forms of social interaction.

The process of the rise of the self-regulating market system was not an even and continuous process. Simplifying matters somewhat, it appears that the markets in land and money were established approximately half a century prior to the development of the market in labour. This delayed development of the labour market did not occur because change in labour institutions was forestalled, but because for a time changes were made in the labour institutions precisely in order to maintain the existing order. Polanyi states on the subject:

> In England both land and money were mobilized before labor was. The latter was prevented from forming a national market by strict legal restrictions on its physical mobility, since the laborer was practically bound to his parish. The Act of Settlement of 1662, which laid down the rules of so-called parish serfdom, was loosened only in 1795. This step would have made possible the setting up of a national labor market had not in the very same year the Speenhamland Law or "allowance system" been introduced. The tendency of this law was to the opposite; namely towards a powerful reinforcement of the paternalistic system of labor organization as inherited from the Tudors and Stuarts.[9]

In Polanyi's analysis change is not simply synonymous with disembedding. The Speenhamland system constituted a new set of rules that in operation created a national wage scale. Overall, the changes in the rules and institutions of labour access were done within the ethic of the Elizabethan labour policy, and not in accordance with the ascendant market ethic. The rules of labour access became market rules only in 1834 when the Speenhamland system was abolished, and the market ethic replaced the Elizabethan ethic. One can distinguish between the changing of rules within the context of an existing valuing-process — the Speenhamland Law in 1795 — and the creation of new rules in the context of new valuing-processes (or of a new ethic) — the repeal of the Speenhamland Law in 1834.

The idea of disembedding can be applied similarly to other cases of change. The discussion, description, and analysis of the processes of change constitute one commonality shared by economic history and economic anthropology. Polanyi's concept of a process of disembedding provides a framework for distinguishing among patterns of change. Alterations in the institutional structure of a society that involve the reorganizing of activities in accordance with a new ethic change the embedding of livelihood in society; these alterations mark a change that results in the decline or collapse of a social and livelihood system. All change involves a shift in material culture or shift in institutional arrangements, but unless the change involves the disembedding or re-embedding of the institutional structure, the changes are accomplished within and through the same social processes. The initial system of livelihood may be changed, but the changes may occur within the context of the on-going ethical system.

### Change and Maori Livelihood

I would now apply Polanyi's concept of degrees of embeddedness to the Maori, the Polynesian natives of New Zealand. In keeping with Polanyi's analytic approach, the analysis of the pattern of change in Maori livelihood will begin with the Maori valuing-process or ethic. Maori valuing will provide the context within which the processes of change engendered by the introduction of white potatoes and firearms will be analyzed. This analysis will be contrasted to the cultural disintegration model of change presented by many New Zealand and Maori scholars.

*Maori Valuing*

The processes of traditional Maori livelihood were based on the principle of *utu*, or reciprocity. The principle required individual Maori either to return all positively and negatively valued actions with similar actions, or to undertake a reversal of relations. Examples of negatively valued actions are insults, bewitching, violation of a *tapu* (ritually restricted access), injury, adultery, and the trespassing of boundaries. Positively valued actions include gifts, feasts, military support, and the effective work of experts and priests. The *utu* for an action depended on the relative status of the parties involved, the degree of kinship, and the past relations between the two parties. The delivery of appropriate *utu* for an action could be delayed until the appropriate return, either positive or negative, could be mustered. The oral histories that were passed from generation to generation were in part an accounting of the positively valued and negatively valued actions that had been done to and by the tribe, clan, family, or individual. The lack of return for either a positively or negatively valued action diminished the status of the tribe, clan, family, or individual.[10] The principle of *utu* applied equally to all acts, whether social, political, economic, or religious. Both purposeful and accidental actions were subject to the same consideration.

The principle of *utu* was both reflexive and transformable. Reflexive, because the relations in which the father was engaged were passed on to the son and his heirs. So, too, were the relations engaged in by the tribe and clan. Relations were on going across generations. The discharge of *utu* by one party creates an obligation of return on the part of the recipient. The principle was transformable, because negative relations could be transformed into positive relations by the appropriate *utu*. Within a tribe, *muru* — the ritual plundering of an individual — would serve as *utu* for any negatively valued action, and transform the intra-tribal relations back to positive. The size of the *muru* raiding party, and the volume of the goods taken, would be indicators of the status of the individual who committed the negatively valued action. The greater in size both of these were, the higher the status. Between tribes, feasts of peace could transform negative relations into peaceful positive relations.

*Utu* as a principle of action united both negatively and positively valued actions into a single valuing system or continuum of valuing. Goods and services were only one of the possible positive forms of *utu*. This contrasts sharply with the valuing structures of self-regulating market systems, where goods are valued independently of other relations between parties involved in the transaction (and only positively at that). Under market rules in economic theory, all demanders are charged the same price: that is, economic interactions are *independent of other* political, social and religious affiliations between the parties. This relationship has been codified into law: if a cashier charges a friend too little for a commodity, he or she can be prosecuted for theft. In Maori economy the distance and strength of the relations were important in establishing the appropriate return. Maori economic activity was thus, in Polanyi's sense, submerged or embedded in the broader social context. The embeddedness of their economic activity is evident in our inability to separate what we would classify as economic behaviour from what we regard as behaviour covered by different sets of ethical rules. But the contrast between Maori valuing and market-system valuing can be found in the valuing processes used. The reflexive and transformable nature of Maori relations has no parallel in market systems.

## White Potatoes and the Maori

The introduction of white potatoes late in the eighteenth century had the most far-reaching impact of all the European introductions. Prior to the introduction of white potatoes, traditionally cultivated vegetables were grown in relatively small amounts, and were consumed only occasionally. The primary cultivated foodstuff of the Maori was the sweet potato.[11] The sweet potato, though the most prolific of the foodstuffs introduced by the Maori to New Zealand, was restricted in its range of cultivation, and for climatic reasons could be grown only with difficulty even in the most favourable areas.[12] The main source of dietary vegetable matter for the Maori was the fern root,[13] which grew wild throughout most of New Zealand.

The small volume of sweet potatoes, and other cultivated foodstuffs, is not indicative of the important role that they had in tribal status. Sweet potatoes were considered to be food for chiefs, and saved for feasts or important visits. The cultivated foodstuffs were part of inter-tribal relations. Chiefs regularly visited other tribes with whom on-going positive relations were maintained. Part of the hospitality given to the visiting chief and members of the expedition was cultivated foodstuffs. This was considered necessary as part of the appropriate display for a chief, and its omission could lead to belligerency. Feasting was also important for inter-tribal relations, and the feast occasioned the consumption of large quantities of cultivated and prepared foods. The display of hospitality, including lavish quantities of the most prized foodstuffs, reflected directly on the status of the tribe and its chief. Thus the role of agricultural activities in the Maori economy was to produce highly valued foodstuffs that were consumed on special occasions for the display of tribal status.

The introduction of European garden vegetables dramatically changed the role of cultivation in Maori society. The white potato was more prolific than the sweet potato because it proved better suited to the temperate climate of New Zealand and was by all measures easier to produce on a seasonal basis. On both the North and South Islands white potatoes were harvested twice a year while sweet potatoes could be harvested only once in the best districts; in the most populated areas white potatoes were grown year-round.[14] The seasonal advantage of the white potato was that it required fewer days between killing frosts to grow: the white potato required between 100 and 110 days to mature,[15] while the sweet potato required 150 or more.[16] After its introduction, the white potato spread rapidly throughout New Zealand and was used by the Maori as a substitute consumable for sweet potatoes in feasting and for hospitality.

The use of white potatoes as a tribal consumable generated a series of changes. The most dramatic was to the respective roles of men, women and slaves in tribal production. Sweet potatoes were planted and harvested only by men of status observing strict field *tapu*. Women did not participate in the activities because they were without *tapu*. If they entered the cultivations, touched any instruments utilized, or came into contact with the men under *tapu* for cultivations, the protective field *tapu* would be polluted and the success of the sweet potato crop would be jeopardized. White potatoes, in contrast, could be cultivated by women and slaves, that is by those of low or no status. According to recorded tribal histories the first white potatoes were cultivated by men,[17] but early in the nineteenth century cultivation became the task of women.[18] The tribal and household production of cultivated foodstuffs shifted from being solely dependent on men of status to being a function of the number of low-status individuals of the tribe. Women and slaves became, in effect, agricultural labourers. This major change in the role of women and slaves in tribal livelihood would have a major impact on other aspects of Maori society.

*Firearms and White Potatoes*

The introduction of firearms to New Zealand in conjunction with the *tapu*-free cultivations generated changes in slavery and warfare. The *tapu*-free cultivation of the white potato transformed slaves into active contributors to the livelihood of the tribe and thus the objective of warfare shifted. Prior to the introduction of white potatoes, the objective was to kill men of status, but as slaves and women became more involved in producing white potatoes, the capturing of slaves became more important.[19] Prior to the adoption of white potatoes there were few slaves,[20] but in the decades following the introduction of white potatoes, the number of slaves grew significantly.

The rise in long-distance warfare for the capture of slaves was synchronous with the adoption of firearms by the Maori. Maori scholars have associated the beginning of annual long-distance warfare with the carrying of firearms by war parties. Long-distance warfare "resulted from the fact that a warlike people was suddenly given — and seized upon — an improved means of expressing its warlike nature."[21] In battle "the musket replaced the spear and club"[22] with the result that a "complete revolution came about in fighting methods."[23] Firearms fuelled the violent proclivity of the Maori, and "destroyed the very fabric of Maori society."[24] This model of the disembedding and collapse of Maori society is based on two invalid assumptions: first, that firearms were used in warfare to kill the enemy; and second, that firearms replaced *all* traditional Maori weapons in warfare, and thus were the basic cause of change in traditional Maori warfare patterns.

As I observed earlier, the objective of warfare changed to the capture of slaves, and indeed, the Maori used the musket to further that objective. However, the Maori used their new firearms not to kill their enemies, but rather only to strike fear in them. Traditional Maori battles had three phases: distant attack, close combat, and finally the pursuit. In pre-musket warfare spears and other distant weapons were rarely fatal or otherwise decisive.[25] The crucial battle action was hand-to-hand combat using war clubs where the actual close-in battle was of relatively short duration. The fall of the first warrior or of an important chief would often cause the fallen man's group to retreat and subsequently be pursued by the victors.[26] The pursuit was actually the most fatal phase in pre-musket warfare,[27] but when muskets replaced spears in long-range warfare, the nature of warfare changed, for the use of firearms was not based on hitting a target, but on the fear the arms generated. When two tribes would meet in battle, the one with fewer firearms would flee, fearing the power of the other. Not only would fleeing warriors be pursued, but also the women and children of the defeated tribe. Muskets, therefore, effectively eliminated hand-to-hand combat. In general, battles in which firearms were used were "not bloody."[28] Up until 1840, European residents and visitors to New Zealand noted the inability of the Maori to shoot firearms accurately.[29] A Sydney paper carried a trader's account of the siege of a Maori fort in 1832. One of his companions canoed out to a trade vessel "amidst showers of musketry,"[30] and returned under "continual firing from the beach. Mr. Love had a very narrow escape, having to land in the midst of it; but fortunately, the New Zealanders are very bad marksmen."[31] This incompetency, however, was not important to the Maori, for the objective was the creation of fear, not the killing of the enemy. The lack of casualties in musket warfare led at least one chief to decry its use:

> My old friend had a great hatred for the musket. He said that in battles fought with the musket there were never so many men killed as when, in his young days, men fought hand to hand with the spear; when a good warrior would kill six, eight, ten, or even twenty men in a single fight; for, when once the enemy broke and commenced to run, the combatants being so close together, a fast runner would knock a dozen on the head in a short time; and the great aim of these fast-running warriors, of whom my old friend had been one, was to chase straight on and never stop, only striking one blow at a man, so as to cripple him, so that those behind should be sure to overtake and finish him.[32]

Thus, by 1840, the Maori use of muskets had made warfare less deadly, and the warfare itself had become focused on the acquisition of slaves.[33]

## White potatoes, Warfare and Inter-tribal Relations

The changes in the range and in the size of war parties were not associated with the use of firearms in warfare, but with the adoption of white potatoes. The higher yield of white potatoes led to an increase in the ability of tribes to conduct inter-tribal relations — both positive (peaceful) and negative (belligerent). The scale and regularity of feasting increased after the introduction of white potatoes, and local warfare declined because feasts were employed to offset negatively valued actions that could lead to warfare. In any case, feasts could also be used to build positive relations. By contrast, long-distance warfare, which had been quite infrequent prior to the introduction of white potatoes, began to be conducted regularly. The war parties were gathered by feasts of war. The freeing of men of status from cultivation obligations resulted in a shift in the time component of warfare. The adoption of white potatoes not only allowed the size of war parties to increase, as larger war parties could be established by larger feasts, but also allowed war parties to be absent for longer periods of time — that is, away conducting warfare at a greater distance. Prior to the arrival of white potatoes, the limit on the time component of warfare was the time between the planting and the harvesting of sweet potatoes. The warriors of the war parties were also the men of status required for the cultivation of the sweet potatoes. The elimination of cultivation as a male activity and increased local peacefulness thus allowed the pursuit of long-distance warfare.

Long-distance warfare, however, was only part of the expanding frontier of regular inter-tribal relations, both positive and negative. At the same time that tribes were warring against distant tribes, they were engaging in positive relations with the neighbours of their distant enemies. Long-distance expeditions often obtained assistance from local allies. If the defeat was considered to have provided sufficient satisfaction, defeated tribes were transformed into allies. The range of traditional relations increased in distance due to the greater ability to conduct those relations at a distance. The rise of regular long-distance warfare was the negative aspect of the changing frontier of relations among the Maori. Thus, the range of gift relations expanded, and the objective of the tribe remained focused on status.

### A New View of Causes and Effects

To traditional scholars the rise of long-distance firearms warfare among the Maori was a dominant force in the disintegration of traditional Maori society. The aggressive tendencies of the Maori were unleashed by the acquisition of firearms. The result was a disruption of the traditional system. That argument ignores the ways in which Maori society valued and adapted the new technologies. Firearms and white potatoes changed the roles of men, women and slaves in Maori society, but did so within the context of Maori valuing. On the surface the Maori-collapse argument is an ethnocentric approach to innovation and technology, implying that only Western societies can adjust to external innovation. The obverse of that is the view of non-Western societies as fixed systems, with all deviations seen as inherently disintegrative. In fact new technologies and new opportunities led to a recasting of roles but not to a breakdown of order.

White potatoes were simultaneously changing the roles of men, women, and slaves in tribal livelihood. White potatoes could be cultivated by women and slaves. This freed men to conduct warfare for longer periods of time and over greater distances. The rise in the size and frequency of war parties was the consequence of these expanding cultivations and increased quantities of cultivated foodstuffs. The change from killing to capturing the enemy reflected the changing role of slaves in tribal livelihood.

Paralleling the increase in the role of women and slaves in cultivation and the decline in the role of men in cultivation was the rise of a new role for men, that of conducting relations with a wider range of tribes. Maori tribes translated increasing quantities of potatoes into a wider range of regular relations. Warfare was only one aspect of the changing of relations at a distance.

The changes in Maori livelihood and social process generated by European goods and technology were adaptations within the context of traditional Maori valuing. Livelihood had changed, but was not disembedded from Maori society. Although he never wrote anything about the Maori, Karl Polanyi's concept of disembedding is a potent tool for the delineating of economic and social change. The analysis of change in the context of embeddedness can distinguish between the recasting of society in the context of a different ethic, and the re-ordering of social process as a response to new opportunities within an ongoing cultural system.

## Notes

1. Fagan 1984. This book makes the cultural collapse argument for a wide range of Western contact histories.
2. Sinclair 1959; Wright 1959; Cumberland 1950.
3. Sinclair 1959, 41.
4. Wright 1959, 192.
5. Cumberland 1950, 33–34.
6. Polanyi 1944.
7. Polanyi 1944, 46.
8. Polanyi 1944, 71.
9. Polanyi 1944, 77–78.
10. Metge 1976, 15; Firth 1972, 412–13.
11. Bellwood 1978, 36, 111.
12. Yen 1961, 340–42.
13. Banks 1963, 19; Savage 1973 [1807], 8–9.
14. Polack 1978 [1840], 1.194.
15. Grubb and Guilford 1912, 27.
16. Simmons 1969, 27.
17. White 1890, 153–54.
18. Marsden, in Elder 1934, 23; Elder 1932, 113.
19. Polack 1978 [1840], 2.36.
20. Banks 1963, 32–34; Cr. Anderson in Cook 1967, 251–52; Clesmeur in McNab 1914, 75.
21. Wright 1959, 81.
22. Wright 1959, 145.
23. Keesing 1928, 42.
24. Fagan 1984, 257–58.
25. Vayda 1960, 8–9.
26. Vayda 1960, 8, 26–28; Buck 1966, 398, 400.
27. Maning 1963 [1863], 194.
28. Fairfowl in McNab 1908, 557.
29. Cruise 1974 [1824], 281–82; Yate 1970 [1835], 112–13, 127; Cruik 1830, 254.
30. McNab 1975 [1913], 51.
31. McNab 1975 [1913], 51.
32. Maning 1963 [1863], 174.

33. Polack 1978 [1840], 2.2, 9–10, 16–17, 21, 22, 36, 95–96; Earle 1966 [1832], 92–93; Williams 1867, 138, 160, 188; Cruik 1830, 254; McNab 1975 [1913] 51; Elder 1932, 284; Rogers 1961, 230–40, 257.

## References

Banks, Joseph. 1963. *The Endeavour Journal of Joseph Banks: 1768–1771*, edited by J. C. Beaglehole. Vol. 2. 2d ed. Sydney: Public Library of New South Wales/Angus and Robertson.

Bellwood, Peter S. 1978. *The Polynesians: Prehistory of an Island People.* London: Thames and Hudson.

Buck, Peter H. (Te Rangi Hiroa). 1966. *The Coming of the Maori.* 2d ed. Wellington: Maori Purposes Fund Board/Whitcombe and Tombs.

Cook, James. 1967. *Captain Cook in New Zealand*, edited by A. W. Reed and A. H. Reed. 2d ed. Wellington: A. W. Reed and A. H. Reed.

Cruik, George L. 1830. *The New Zealanders.* Boston: Lilly and Wait.

Cruise, Richard A. 1974 [1824]. *Journal of a Ten Months' Residence in New Zealand.* 2d ed. London: Longman, Hurst, Rees, Orme, and Brown. Reprint Christchurch: Capper Press.

Cumberland, Kenneth B. 1950. "A Land Despoiled: New Zealand about 1838." *New Zealand Geographer* 6:13–34.

Earle, Augustus. 1966 [1832]. *Narrative of a Nine Months' Residence in New Zealand,* edited by E. H. McCormick. London: Longman, Rees, Orme, Brown, Green, and Longman. Reprint Oxford: Oxford University Press.

Elder, John Rawson, ed. 1932. *The Letters and Journals of Samuel Marsden, 1765–1838.* Dunedin, NZ: Coulls, Somerville, Wilkie/A. H. Reed/Otago University Council.

———, ed. 1934. *Marsden's Lieutenants.* Dunedin, NZ: Coulls, Somerville, Wilkie/A. H. Reed/Otago University Council.

Fagan, Brian M. 1984. *Clash of Cultures.* New York: W. H. Freeman.

Firth, Raymond. 1972. *Economics of the New Zealand Maori.* 2d ed. Wellington: Government Printer.

Grubb, E. H., and W. S. Guilford. 1912. *The Potato.* New York: Doubleday, Page.

Keesing, Felix M. 1928. *The Changing Maori.* Memoirs of the Board of Maori Ethnological Research, Vol. 4. New Plymouth, NZ: Thomas Avery and Sons.

Maning, Frederick. 1963 [1863]. *Old New Zealand.* London: Smith, Elder and Co. Reprint Auckland: Whitcombe and Tombs.

McNab, Robert, ed. 1908, 1914. *Historical Records of New Zealand.* 2 vols. Wellington: A. R. Shearer.

———. 1975 [1913]. *The Old Whaling Days: A History of Southern New Zealand from 1830 to 1840*. Christchurch: Whitcomb and Tombs. Reprint Auckland: Golden Press.
Metge, Joan. 1976. *The Maori of New Zealand: Rautahi*. Rev. ed. London: Routledge and Kegan Paul.
Polack, Joel Samuel. 1978 [1840]. *Manners and Customs of the New Zealanders*. 2 vols. London: J. Madden. Reprint New York: AMS Press.
Polanyi, Karl. 1944. *The Great Transformation*. New York: Holt Rinehart and Winston.
Rogers, Lawrence M., ed. 1961. *The Early Journals of Henry Williams: 1826–1840*. Christchurch: Pegasus.
Savage, John. 1973 [1807]. *Some Account of New Zealand, Particularly the Bay of Islands and Surrounding Country*. London: J. Murray. Reprint Christchurch: Capper Press.
Simmons, David. 1969. "Economic Change in New Zealand Prehistory." *Journal of the Polynesian Society* 78:3–34.
Sinclair, Keith. 1959. *A History of New Zealand*. Harmondsworth: Penguin.
Vayda, A. P. 1960. *Maori Warfare*. Polynesian Society Maori Monographs, no. 2. Wellington: Polynesian Society.
White, John. 1890. *The Ancient History of the Maori, His Mythology and Traditions*. Vol. 5. Wellington: Government Printer.
Williams, William. 1867. *Christianity among the New Zealanders*. London: Seeley, Jackson, and Halliday.
Wright, Harrison M. 1959. *New Zealand, 1769–1840: Early Years of Western Contact*. Cambridge, MA: Harvard University Press.
Yate, William. 1970 [1835]. *An Account of New Zealand*. 2d ed. London: R. B. Seeley and W. Burnside. Reprint Shannon: Irish University Press, 1970.
Yen, D. E. 1961. "The Adaptation of Kumara by the New Zealand Maori." *Journal of the Polynesian Society* 70:338–48.

# 8

## Exposure and Protection: The Double Movement in the Economic History of Rural India*

### Walter C. Neale

Central to Karl Polanyi's analysis of the nineteenth century was the double movement: a continuous expansion of the market system and simultaneously a "countermovement ... a reaction against dislocation which attacked the fabric of society." Each side of the double movement set "itself specific institutional aims" and enjoyed "the support of definite social forces." Economic liberalism aimed "at the establishment of a self-regulating market, relying on the support of the trading classes ...." On the other side, a movement for social protection was devoted to man and nature as well as to productive organization. It relied on the support of those most immediately affected by the deleterious action of the market, and its methods were protective legislation, restrictive associations, and other instruments of intervention. Class was important. "The middle classes were the bearers of the nascent market economy .... To the landed aristocracy and the peasantry fell the task of safeguarding ... men and soil, while the laboring people, to a smaller or greater extent, became representatives of the common human interests .... But at one time or

---

* *The author is indebted to Kathleen Brown, Anne Mayhew, and David W. Tandy for careful readings and thoughtful suggestions; and to Karl Polanyi for the concept of the double movement, to the British Empire for much of the information upon which this paper is based, and to the citizens of India who have institutionalized the freedoms that were so important to Polanyi. The ideas in this paper, the first part of which draws largely on Neale 1962, were originally presented at the second International Karl Polanyi Conference, held in Montréal in November 1988.*

another, each social class stood, even if unconsciously, for interests wider than its own."[1]

In India there have been two double movements: one, largely in respect of land, during the nineteenth century, and another, largely in respect of rural labour, during the second half of the twentieth century. (More instances of double movements in India may be identified; I shall deal only with the two with which I am familiar.) During the nineteenth century, in what is known as UP (the United Provinces of Agra and Oudh, in northern India), the British themselves adopted two sets of policies that in some respects were analogous to the double movement in nineteenth-century Britain but in other respects strikingly different.[2]

The policies were analogous in that the British rulers introduced a self-regulating market system and in that a series of regulations and laws were enacted to protect the peasantry from the effects of the system.

The policies were strikingly different in a number of ways. The East India Company's introduction of the self-regulating market system was not part of a plan to change the Indian economy — as free trade, enclosure acts, Poor Law reform, and the Bank Charter Act were clearly conscious efforts to change the British economy. Rather, it was a result of accepted assumptions about the nature of the world.

The growth in the power of the market owed more to the adaptations of the superior landholding groups to the new markets than it did to political activity. Adaptation to the market was a product of two rather inconsistent reactions of the landholding castes: their desire to maintain dominance in village politics, and their desire to reap the gains of the new system. There seems to have been a transition from an early stage — in the late eighteenth and early nineteenth centuries, when holders of large areas did not yet appreciate the gains that British ideas of title and market made possible — to the view that there need be no restraints upon how one took advantage of these possibilities. One is reminded of J. S. Furnivall's characterization of the situation in colonial dependencies: "So far as the people are released from customary inhibitions, economic forces are subject to no restraint but that of Western law. In the West the law is an expression of social will .... But in the tropics Western law is imposed by society from outside, and, because it is not an expression of social will, it is powerless to restrain anti-social economic forces."[3] Indian landlords, when they had grasped the rules (but had not adopted the Western ethics) of the market system, pushed the logic of market gain beyond what the British themselves had done at home. In the middle decades of the nineteenth century Indian landlords had become thoroughgoing rent-maximizers, while many British administrators had become more "pro-tenant" than had any of their peers at home.

The efforts to protect — first the "rightful" owners of land in their continued possession and later the tenants — were actions of the same Company (and the successor Imperial) authorities that had introduced the self-regulating market. This dual role — from both sides of the double movement — was not the result of a change of mind, but of being of two minds about the policies that should be pursued. The British administrators did not all change their minds; rather, a new emphasis was emerging. As early as 1819, Holt Mackenzie, a senior civil servant appointed by the government of Bengal to investigate the tenure system that had existed in the UP districts, argued that tenants' customary rents be protected.[4] In 1844, occupancy rights were effectively (but not legislatively) granted to some classes of tenants in UP by administrative *Directions to Settlement Officers* and *Directions for Collectors*.[5] The Bengal Presidency, via Bengal Act X of 1859, granted occupancy rights to tenants who had farmed the same land for twelve years. Yet from that date until 1864 there was controversy between Sir John Lawrence, governor of UP, and Sir Charles Wingfield, chief commissioner of Oudh (a part of UP), the governor rejecting the commissioner's insistence upon granting the *talukdars* (landlords) of Oudh unrestricted proprietary rights. Throughout, one set of minds was increasingly rejecting market solutions, the other supporting them; in the end, the former group dominated policy.

The landed classes (*zamindars, talukdars*) were a "liberalizing" force by virtue of their actions, but at no time did they articulate a position in respect of the market. Until the time of the Independence Movement after World War I, the tenantry played little role, and the labouring classes played no role at all. During the 1930s tenants conducted a No Rent campaign corresponding to the landlords' No Revenue campaign, both organized by Mohandas K. Gandhi and the Indian National Congress as part of the Independence Movement. In addition, during the 1920s and 1930s a number of peasant organizations (kisan sabhas) were formed; these were the first associations organized by people whose security had been threatened or destroyed by the market, but they did not change the pattern or direction already set.[6]

During the years since independence there has been another double movement, now spreading throughout India. This time, the counter movement, again primarily government-sponsored, has, like the counter movement in Britain a century ago, consisted of specific efforts to protect specific groups exposed to the insecurities of the self-regulating market. As was the case in the nineteenth century, governments have not been in complete agreement; but again there have been marked contrasts to the British case: this time, powerful market forces were inadvertently created by way of land reforms and government development programmes. Both programmes were well planned and thoroughly articulated, but there was not the slightest intention of creating a self-regulating market. In fact, the programmes were introduced by socialist governments that had every intention of intervening in markets.

From the 1960s through the 1980s class did play a role on both sides of the double movement; but on neither side was there a drive to "free" the market or to enact specific reforms. Rather, on the one side, an emerging class of owner-operator farmers strengthened the market by virtue of how they managed their farms. On the other side, landless labourers were beginning to exercise power through the ballot and the riot; but it was the government that devised policies to protect labour from the actions of the owner-operators.

### The Double Movement, 1800–1939

Just what the civil servants of the East India Company thought about Indian land tenures in 1800 is not clear; they did believe that someone must own the land, that the owner of the land had a right to the net revenue from the land, and that the ruler (*raja*, emperor) was the owner. When they first assessed the "revenue demand" (the amount to be paid to the ruler), they certainly assessed as if the owner (the Company) could and should maximize its receipts, and they certainly treated those responsible for paying the revenue demand as if they were tenants by the year. (The assignment of responsibility was called the "settlement" of the revenue demand; the settlement effectively granted power of ownership to the person with whom the settlement was made for the period of the settlement — in UP, at that time, five years.)

The civil servants who managed the Bengal Presidency over the next three decades simply *assumed* that an "Anglo-Roman" system of property existed everywhere in the world, that a self-regulating market was normal and natural, and that the return to the owner was and should be what we have come to call the "Ricardian rent." There was no interest or class in a position to raise doubts or argue that the assumptions were wrong.

Thus the struggle to impose the market that marked British history from the *Wealth of Nations* through Speenhamland to Poor Law reform and repeal of the Corn Laws was absent in India — absent as an intellectual struggle and absent as a political struggle. The legal framework of the self-regulating market system sprang fully grown from the unconscious of the Company. But if there were no classes or interest groups in a position to articulate objections, there were troubles enough for the administrators: widespread failure to collect revenues led to re-settlement with people who were members neither of the original landed classes nor of cultivating castes; and civil servants in the area reported that dissatisfaction and resentment were growing.

The first steps toward "self-protection" were not "self" but official in provenance. In 1819, Holt Mackenzie reported that Indian ideas of tenure were radically different from any British conceptions.[7] He argued that there was rarely a single proprietor of a piece of land or of a village, that the Company often settled with *representatives* of a group of proprietors and that these representatives should never be treated as owners. Mackenzie, however, did not discuss the rights of the lower levels of rural society; his purpose was to protect former landholders from those who had been *rajas* before the British conquest and from an emerging class of revenue farmers. (Two years later a commission was established to annul transfers of land that appeared to have been inequitable, and many of the dispossessed became repossessed of their land. The extension of official protection down through the layers of tenancy was a long, slow process. It has begun to reach the landless only during the last two decades.)

One mark of a double movement is that it is not a sequence — first a self-regulating market, then a protective reaction — but a synchronic movement on both sides, dating from introduction of the self-regulating market. In Britain, Luddites and Chartists were active just as Parliament was introducing, step by step, a self-regulating market. The history of UP is similar. As the first step toward official protection was being taken, the government was moving toward a more British system of proprietorship. Section 1 of Regulation VII of 1822 stated that whereas a moderate assessment being equally conducive to the true interests of Government ... the efforts of the revenue officers should be chiefly directed ... [to] the objects of equalizing the public burthens, and of ascertaining, settling, and recording the rights ... of all persons and classes, owning, occupying, managing, or cultivating the land, or gathering or disposing of its produce, or collecting or appropriating the rent or revenue payable on account of land ....[8]

Regulation VII mixed both sides of the double movement — peculiarly, one might think, but consistently with the peculiarity that both sides of the double movement were official. Limiting the revenue demand gave landholders a net income, thus granting more substance of ownership and changing the revenue demand from a rent to a tax. By recording rights in land it reduced the possibility of fraud and thus gave greater security of tenure to those with whom the settlement was made. On the other hand, by recording the rights of some classes of tenants it began the process of recognizing the layers of other rights beneath those of the primary owner and limiting the substance of the property it created. On balance, Regulation VII did more to create a self-regulating market than it did to limit such a market.

However, as tax law it could not be administered. From 1800 to 1821 it was assumed that the revenue was a Ricardian rent. After 1821 it was assumed that the taxable incomes of the *zamindar* (the superior holder) was a Ricardian rent, meaning gross income less costs. But costs were at best implicit, and in fact embedded in the village system — in customary rents, in rents in kind, in family labour, and in all the obligations of the dominant and landholding castes to support the village artisans, servants, and priests with shares from the harvest.[9] In the absence of a capital market (the moneylending operations of landholders and moneylenders could hardly be called a capital market), there was no way to cost the tools, dikes, wells, and irrigation channels. Within ten years the settlement officers (the civil servants who made the settlements) were saying that it would take sixty years to compute net rents, by which time all the earlier computations would be outdated.[10] Implicit Ricardian rent had become explicit; and Ricardian rent was proving an impossible basis for taxation.

The term Ricardian rent does not enter economic literature until 1815 — actually with Robert Thomas Malthus. The ideas of the classical economists became popular, in some areas even dominant, among the Company's civil servants, but explicit references by the civil servants to the economists occur only after 1817 or 1820. However, something very like the classical concept of rent seems to have dominated Company thought from an earlier date. To what degree and from what date the Company's civil servants were using the ideas of the classical economists — in whatever form they may have articulated the ideas — must remain a matter of conjecture. In 1805 Malthus had been appointed to the chair of political economy at Haileybury College, where the Company's civil servants-to-be were trained before going out to India. Many may have absorbed the classical assumptions during their training. It is quite possible that Malthus was professing his ideas well before 1815, or even that the idea of differential rent was "in the air" before Malthus formalized it. It should be noted that the civil servants increasingly held that the net differential rent should be regarded as a ceiling upon revenue demand, not the amount that the Company should try to extract.[11]

The Company's solution to the problem of how high the revenue demand should be was Section 2 of Regulation IX of 1833: "So much of Regulation VII of 1822 as prescribes or has been understood to prescribe, that the amount of *jumma* [revenue] to be demanded from any *mehaul* [estate] shall be calculated on an ascertainment of the quantity and value of actual produce, or on a comparison between the costs of production and value of the produce, is hereby rescinded."[12] Historical rents replaced conceptual rents less conceptual costs. This change resulted in further unplanned interventions in the market. There was so much difficulty over the next two decades in determining what the historical rents actually were that it became common practice for the settlement officers to use their judgement. Rents were increasingly becoming market-determined; but a principle-in-practice was established that officials could be the ultimate determiners of rents.

The history of the next 100 years is a story of the gradual replacement of rental markets for land by official determination of "fair" rents. The major landmarks were the Bengal Act X of 1859, which provided heritable occupancy rights to tenants who had cultivated the same plot for twelve years;[13] the Great Rent Case, in which the High Court of Bengal held that rents of tenants on indigo lands could be enhanced only in proportion to the rise in the price of indigo;[14] the development of the "seven years' rule" in the late nineteenth century, which established the principle that rents could be enhanced only after seven years and by no more than one sixteenth; and a series of acts in the 1920s and 1930s that granted hereditary rights to a majority of tenants. These landmarks were only the most striking of numerous acts that amended the law or the procedures that interpreted it, most tending to limit the rights of owners against their tenants until, in 1939, Act XVII virtually abolished the rental market for land.[15] The post-independence Zamindari Abolition Act only fulfilled the logic implicit in the earlier policies, making most cultivators (but not farm labourers) tenants of the state.[16]

What has been described here was official policy, but actual administration fell far short of intent. Local powers could always threaten violence, and the administration did not have the financial and human resources nor the moral authority to enforce the law effectively. Thus what is described should be read as an increasingly effective tendency, rather than as what was actually happening at any time in the villages.

There was an inherent logic to the official protective movement. If the actual tenant cultivators were to be protected by the granting of secure tenancies, then the government had to fix the rents that the tenants would pay: otherwise large enhancements of rent would have served to evict cultivators who had been granted occupancy rights. This logic led to the granting of rent-fixing powers to settlement officers — powers limiting the rights of property and so the power of the market — and eventually to abolition of the rental market.

At no time during this period did the British perceive themselves to be "changing sides." The shift from a "liberal," pro-market, pro-property position to a protective, interventionist one was perceived by the British rulers as protecting equitable rights in property (and, increasingly, the equitable property rights of tenants). In undertaking the role of protector of social stability — the role of aristocratic landlords and the farm population in Britain's double movement — the British rulers of India saw no inconsistency with their faith in property and markets.

In India, the same ruling classes, the same people, the same minds articulated each side of the double movement. In Britain, it was as if each group and class affected by the self-regulating system found itself thinking, "We cannot operate unless institutions are changed to allow us to fulfil our roles in our economy and society." In India it was as if many British administrators, having established the legal and institutional framework for the market, found themselves thinking, "We cannot fulfil our roles as protectors of property, as collectors of taxes, and as guarantors of social stability unless we change the laws and regulations under which we operate." In Britain groups articulated demands that filled the needs of many other groups; in India it was a single group — composed of people with marked differences of opinion, often in conflict, but united in a single administration governed by the decisions that emerged from the administrative hierarchy.

In this history the role of the superior landholders was quite different from what it had been in Britain. At first unfamiliar with the working of a market system — but hardly unfamiliar with a multitude of ways in which to exploit the lower orders of society — they slowly learned how to use the opportunities provided by the new system. To what degree they learned to use the opportunities in order to increase their money incomes is not clear. Before the British conquest there had not been many opportunities to spend income on consumer or capital goods; few such goods were produced to be bought. (Major improvements to be made on the land — wells, erosion dikes, percolation ponds, irrigation channels — were most easily constructed by local, dependent labourers, and they usually were.) British conquest and rule did not provide much more in the way of manufactured goods. Industrialization did not begin in India until the 1850s, and then primarily to produce lower quality textiles. A wider range of goods began to be produced around 1900; but despite the fact that by the 1930s India became, next to Japan, the Third World's major producer of industrial goods, output remained small, especially in proportion to population. Much the same can be said of industrially produced goods imported from Britain: these increased, but the volume was never proportionate to the population; the textile imports of historical fame were those purchased by the lower orders (who also bought the output of the Indian textile industry). Thus seizing opportunities to maximize monetary gain on the market was not so obviously rewarded by things to buy, while the joys of being a "big man" in a village (a big fish in small pond, a *bura sahib*) remained attractive and possible.

The opportunities created by British ideas about property and the role of property in markets helped the landholding classes to keep their power locally. The landlords became increasingly sophisticated in manipulating the judicial processes. The courts were used to harry tenants. In Britain people were loyal to their system of courts and obeyed its rules because the system and the rules were part of their own culture. But there was no reason for the Indians to feel loyalty to British courts and procedures; and British court processes had little to do with Indian ideas of how to settle disputes. In the absence of respect for the courts, Indian loyalties to family, faction, and caste made it inevitable that there would be chicanery outside and perjury within the courts. The rich and powerful could falsify more records and marshal or bribe more witnesses than could the poor and powerless. Thus eviction suits without merit could be used to exhaust the resources of recalcitrant tenants; even the threat of a suit could bring a tenant to heel. Tenants with legitimate cases dared not bring them. Similarly, suits and threats of suits over matters of the peasants' debts served to assure compliance.[17]

The increasing efforts of the British administration to protect the peasantry were in significant measure a response to the effectiveness with which the landholders were adapting to the new order. As the landlords slowly created the market that the British had originally assumed, the British increasingly tried to limit market-determined relationships. It was a race between the British, as they granted rights to former proprietors or adopted the twelve and seven years' rules, and the landlords, as they intensified their efforts to maintain local dominance.

**The Double Movement, 1947–1988**

*Growth of the Market in Rural India*

After 1947 the state governments of independent India undertook to reform their systems of land tenure.[18] Because the systems of tenure in the states varied enormously, so also did the provisions and the timing of the reforms. It would serve no purpose here to attempt to outline these, but I will point to three consequences:

1) Transfers of titles to tenants, and/or ceilings on the amount of land a family could own, meant abolition of the large landholder.

Whereas in 1947 there were *zamindars, talukdars,* and *jagirdars* (kinds of landowners), often owning extensive tracts that could run into thousands of acres, by the 1960s a person with fifty acres was considered a large landowner. While the majority of landowners held less than two acres, most of the arable land was held by owner-operators farming economically viable holdings ranging from two or three to fifteen or twenty acres. In these circumstances the level of rents and insecurity of tenure ceased to be pressing issues.

2) Landless labourers gained no titles to land, and some tenants became landless labourers.

3) A land-owning, family-farming peasantry became the dominant class in the Indian countryside.

In the 1950s, and increasingly thereafter, planned development provided India with a wide variety and a substantial quantity of domestically produced consumer and capital goods, a variety as great as one finds in most developed countries. There were things to buy with the greater incomes: at first fountain pens, transistor radios, bicycles, factory-made shoes, and tiled roofs; then pump sets, fertilizers, pesticides, motorcycles, refrigerators, television sets, college educations, and even small cars.

In the late 1960s came the Green Revolution, at first affecting wheat and rice, then extending to the millets, and revolutionizing not only the technology of these crops but also the attitudes of farmers toward all kinds of modern agricultural technology.[19] To illustrate: in the 1950s extension officers had trouble finding a willing audience in the villages; by the 1970s Punjabi farmers were coming to the offices of agronomy professors to ask about the latest developments in scientific farming.[20] (Words of warning are, however, in order here. These changes have been great in the northwest, in Bengal, in the coastal districts of Andhra and Tamil Nadu, and in a few other places. Change is less obvious in the large central area of the Gangetic plain and much of inland southern India, so that my argument does not apply to the entire country.[21])

Independent India is a democracy. The governments at the centre, in the states, and in the localities are elected by secret ballot. The lower orders have been learning to use the immense power of this weapon. In addition, the lower orders, especially the untouchables, have adopted a weapon of the middle orders and the castes: the riot. (It should be understood that the many riots in India are not a sign that the government has lost control and that the world has become dangerous. They are an integral part of India's political system: a signal to the authorities that feelings are running high and that the government should respond. These politically symbolic riots should not be confused with the large-scale communal riots intended to kill and destroy the property of people of another religion, nor with the small-scale beatings and killings of untouchables.) In the 1950s and 1960s untouchables would not have dared to riot; when members of higher castes thrashed an untouchable, there was no response. Now untouchables respond with their own violence. Governments and their administrators heed the signal that they must respond to the demands and frustrations of the lower orders, and they do much more to protect them from the violence, threats, and chicanery of the higher orders.

Owner-operated farming *plus* Green Revolution technology *plus* the availability of market goods *plus* fewer opportunities to use the older means of maintaining local dominance have created a class of "bullock capitalists" (some of whom are becoming "tractor capitalists").[22] As the Green Revolution technology has provided the means to earn incomes to spend on the new goods, it has also required that farmers buy cement or steel tubes for wells, pumps, and fertilizers. With all those outlays sunk in the new technology, the idea of purchasing chemical pesticides can be very attractive.[23] The need to buy inputs combined with the desire to buy the new goods makes market-centred activities much more appealing. At the same time, democratic politics is depriving the landed of the power to use the output of their land to gather factions to dominate their villages and to enjoy the customary subservience of tenants and labourers. Consequently, landless labour has lost the security provided by the old system of local politics and has become dependent upon a market wage. The transformation of peasant farmers into bullock capitalists has given market prices and wages an importance that they had never had before.[24]

Lest the reader understand me to mean that the old system was "good," I emphasize that it provided income security to the subservient at the cost of dignity and opportunity. I know of no evidence that the lower orders would trade their new power and insecurity for their former dependence.

Bullock capitalists are certainly *not* nineteenth-century liberals. They have formed parties, or factions within the Congress Party, to assure themselves of price supports and subsidized inputs. They are hardly averse to government intervention in market processes. Nevertheless, by far the most important effect of their adaptation to the new circumstances has been the creation of a much closer approximation of a self-regulating market than rural India had seen before.

*The Other Side: Whitbread in India*

At the national level there are only bits of evidence that a movement to protect the landless has been building over the last twenty-five years. Indira Gandhi's "Abolish Poverty!" slogan was certainly understood to mean "Do something about the poor, the landless, and the helpless!" The late 1970s saw the introduction of *sarvodaya*, a programme to equip one or a few of the poorest families in each village with the tools, materials, and skills to earn a living independently of the powers-that-be in the village. The parties that have arisen to represent the bullock capitalists have insisted that they represent the interests of the landless. More importantly, state governments have been willing, even eager, to interfere with the operation of the market.[25]

Perhaps the best example of a protective movement in the states is Maharashtra's Employment Guarantee Scheme (EGS). It assures any fifty or more people who present themselves to the District Magistrate (the chief authority in a district) that they will be given work at what was a bit less than the prevailing rural wage. These gangs work largely at manual earth-moving for roads, digging and clearing channels, and building erosion dikes on fields. The scheme is criticized because the workers do not work hard enough (other people never do), because the projects at which they work are not worth the wages paid, and especially because some of the work is done on private land and thus benefits farmers free of charge (the types of criticism that always accompany market interventions). Most striking, however, is the complaint of farmers that they must now pay higher wages, going on double the EGS rates, to get labour that will work hard, long, and conscientiously. Can one think of a better recommendation for the EGS?

In "Why Not Whitbread's Bill?" (a note to his chapter on Speenhamland[26]), Polanyi pointed out that a minimum wage does not destroy the morale of labour or of management and that, unlike guaranteed aid in supplement of wages, a minimum wage does not render rational cost accounting and effective labour management impossible. The EGS has the merits of Whitbread's proposed minimum wage. Furthermore, it not only provides jobs for the landless, it has the added virtue of producing useful things.

These instances are too few to allow the current historian to decide whether the spread of a market-dominated agriculture is being challenged by an effective counter movement; but the evidence is certainly consistent with the emergence of a protective movement throughout India.

Again, there are contrasts to be made with the double movement in Britain. The EGS in Maharashtra is a response to political pressure or at least to concern about the lower orders, and in this respect recalls the politics of nineteenth-century Britain (with the addition that the lower orders in India now vote). However, the manner in which the EGS was introduced resembles the practices of the British imperial administration in India at least if not more than it does those of nineteenth-century Britain.

## Conclusion

The economic history of India provides evidence that double movements have been more widespread than Polanyi appears to have thought, and that their forms and processes may be strikingly different when the social and political systems are different. This history may justify the question: Are double movements integral parts of any evolution of market systems? Perhaps, for instance, scholars should have another look at the economic histories of the countries on the European continent, as the Hungarians of the Budapest School have recently been doing.[27]

Even if the arguments in this paper do not justify such a broad conclusion, the double movements in the history of India present intriguing cases. There, both sides of the earlier double movement originated with the same foreign "governing class," but the moving force developing the market was not a liberal or trading class but a landed class trying to maintain its pre-market dominant position, while the protective movement was a response by the foreign rulers to what they concluded were their own earlier errors. The later double movement does reflect class interests, and again the landed class is a "liberal force" in its actions, if much less so in its intent. And, finally, whether representing a social class or not, each group involved in these histories "stood ... for interests wider than its own."

## Notes

1. This paragraph has paraphrased, plagiarized, and quoted from Polanyi 1944, 130, 132–33.
2. What I argue here is clearly true of the economic history of the United Provinces. Although not generally true of all British India, similarities may be found in the histories of other provinces. (And the argument in the later part of this paper is true of much of India.) The United Provinces began, in 1800, as the Ceded and Conquered Districts, an area shaped rather like a modern telephone and extending from the state of Bihar in the east to the Rajput states, Delhi, and the Punjab in the west. This area then became the North-Western Provinces and, after the annexation of the kingdom of Oudh (giving the province a boot-like shape), became the United Provinces of Agra and Oudh. It has been known as UP ever since. (When India became independent in 1947, the name was changed to Uttar Pradesh — northern state — and people continue to call it UP.) I shall follow common custom and refer to the whole and the parts as UP for the whole period since 1800.

   It should be noted that UP, as part of the Bengal Presidency, was ruled from Calcutta under the British. However, from the 1860s on, legislation and regulations were written specifically for UP and, as will become apparent, from the beginnings in 1800 the policies followed in UP often differed from those followed elsewhere in the Bengal Presidency because the systems of land tenure had been different and became more so.
3. Furnivall 1956, 293.
4. Mackenzie 1886.
5. See Neale 1962, 68, 127.
6. The *talukdars* (large landholders) of Oudh supported the Sepoy Rebellion (Indian Mutiny) of 1857. This support was certainly an organized protest against British policy, but the *talukdars* were protesting their loss of power consequent upon the British occupation in 1855, and were perhaps also protesting the laws and regulations of the North-Western Provinces, which granted some protection to tenants and which were being applied in Oudh. It was *not* a protest against the market, and it is a curious fact that the tenantry in Oudh supported the *talukdars* in the Rebellion. It is best viewed as "the last protest of the old regime."
7. Mackenzie 1886; Thorner 1976 [1956] is certainly the best brief introduction to the general nature of Indian tenures. For those who wish the best and most thorough account for British India through the nineteenth century, there is Baden-Powell 1892. For a brief historical survey, see Neale 1988.
8. Regulation VII of 1822 (in Clarke 1854).
9. The Indian village systems have become known as the *jajmani* system. While descriptions of the systems date back to the Settlement Reports of the nineteenth century, use of this term begins with Wiser and Wiser 1963 [1930] and Wiser 1936, and it is in common use today. During the 1950s, scholars (especially anthropologists) produced a sizeable literature on the topic. Probably the best single item to read is Kolenda 1963. Someone wanting to

read more on the topic might go on to Adams 1970 for a schematic presentation of the elements of Indian village systems; Beidelman 1949 for a quasi-Marxist survey; further, Adams and Woltemade 1970; Adams and Neale 1990.
10. Misra 1942, 64.
11. See Stokes 1959 for an account of the influence of thinking in Britain upon British policy and administration in India, especially 109–16 for the matters discussed here. See also McAlpin 1984 for an account of the dominance of the ideas of the classical economists in the Bombay Presidency. Malthus, not Ricardo, should be credited with the formal articulation of the idea of economic rent since his *Inquiry into the Nature and Progress of Rent* was published in 1815, two years before Ricardo's *Principles of Political Economy and Taxation* (see Wrigley 1988, 101–2, for a brief discussion of who said what when).
12. Regulation IX of 1833, in Clarke 1854.
13. Act X of 1859 ("Bengal Rent Act, 1859"), in Bengal Code 1939.
14. See Campbell 1881, 266–68.
15. Act XVII of 1939 ("U.P. Tenancy Act, 1939"), in U.P. Code 1939.
16. Act I of 1951 ("U.P. Zamindari Abolition and Land Reforms Act, 1950"), in U.P. Code 1951.
17. For descriptions of how courts, social pressures, and power worked, see Carstairs 1912; Cohn 1959; Mason 1946; Moon 1945. I provide a fuller discussion and some additional sources in Neale 1962, 192–208.
18. Thorner 1980 is the best brief account of land reforms in India. Certainly the best full account of land reforms in South Asia is Herring 1983.
19. For these changes as they were emerging in the 1960s, see Thorner 1980, 202–53.
20. The assertion is based upon my experience and observations during field work in Ludhiana and other parts of Punjab during 1956, 1960–61, 1964, 1977, 1978, and 1983.
21. For contrasts between two areas — Punjab, where the Green Revolution transformed agriculture, and Bihar, where there has been little response to the new technologies — see Nair 1979.
22. For the phrase "bullock capitalist" and for an analysis of the politics of this new class, see Rudolph and Rudolph 1980. Leaf (1991) reports that in the Punjab village he has been studying since the mid-1960s tractors have entirely replaced bullocks, some farmers leasing out tractors, others renting them in. However, such instances are probably to be found only in the northwest (in Punjab and Haryana).
23. The correspondence with what happened in the U.S. in the last third of the nineteenth century is striking. See Mayhew 1972; 1990.
24. For a discussion of the changing position of landless labour in general and of untouchables in particular, see Neale 1972. A somewhat longer version of parts of the argument in this section will be found in Neale and Edwards 1983.
25. For an account of the politics of representing and protecting the lower orders in one state, see Manor 1977; 1980.
26. Polanyi 1944, 289–90.
27. Brown 1988, 38–68.

## References

Adams, John. 1970. "Village Economy in Traditional India: A Simplified Model." *Human Organization* 29:49–58.
Adams, John, and Walter C. Neale. 1990. "Indian Village Institutions and Development Policies." In Walter C. Neale, *Developing Rural India: Policies, Politics, and Progress*, 51–61. Riverdale, MD: Riverdale Co.; Bombay: Allied Publishers.
Adams, John, and Uwe J. Woltemade. 1970. "Studies of Indian Village Economies: A Bibliographical Essay." *Indian Economic and Social History Review* 7:109–37.
Baden-Powell, B. H. 1892. *The Land Systems of British India*. Oxford: Clarendon Press.
Beidelman, Thomas O. 1949. *A Comparative Analysis of the Jajmani System*. Locust Valley, NY: J. J. Augustin.
Bengal Code. 1939. *Bengal Code, 1*. 5th ed. Alipore, Bengal: Superintendent, Government Printing.
Brown, Douglas M. 1988. *Towards a Radical Democracy: The Political Economy of the Budapest School*. London: Unwin Hyman.
Campbell, George. 1881. "The Tenure of Land in India." In *Systems of Land Tenure in Various Countries*. Rev. ed. edited by J. W. Probyn for the Cobden Club, 213–89. London: Macmillan.
Carstairs, R. 1912. *The Little World of an Indian District Officer*. London: Macmillan.
Clarke, Richard. 1854. *The Regulations of the Government of Fort William in Bengal, in Force at the End of 1883. Vol. 2, Regulations from 1806 to 1834*. London: J. and H. Cox.
Cohn, Bernard S. 1959. "Some Notes on Law and Change in North India." *Economic Development and Cultural Change* 8:79–93.
Furnivall, J. S. 1956. *Colonial Policy and Practice*. New York: New York University Press.
Herring, Ronald J. 1983. *Land to the Tiller: The Political Economy of Agrarian Reform in South Asia*. New Haven: Yale University Press.
Kolenda, Pauline Mahar. 1963. "Towards a Model of the Hindu Jajmani System." *Human Organization* 22:11–31.
Leaf, Murray J. 1991. "There are no Bullocks in the Village Any More." In *Punjab in Perspective*. South Asia Series, Occasional Paper no. 39, edited by Surjit Dulai and Arthur Helweg, 78–84. East Lansing, Michigan: Asian Studies Center, Michigan State University.
Mackenzie, Holt. 1886. "Memorandum by the Secretary Regarding the Settlements of the Ceded and Conquered Provinces, with Suggestions for the Permanent Settlement of Those Provinces, Dated 1st July 1819." In *Selections from the Revenue Records of the North-West Provinces, 1818–1820*. Calcutta: Military Orphan Press.
Manor, James. 1977. "Structural Change in Karnataka Politics." *Economic and Political Weekly* 12:1865–69.
———. 1980. "Pragmatic Progressives in Regional Politics: The Case of Devraj Urs." *Economic and Political Weekly* 15:201–13.

Mason, Philip [Philip Woodruff, pseud.]. 1946. *Call the Next Witness*. New York: Harcourt Brace.
Mayhew, Anne. 1972. "A Reappraisal of the Causes of Farm Protest in the U.S., 1870–1900." *Journal of Economic History* 32:464–75.
———. 1990. "The Sherman Act as Protective Reaction." *Journal of Economic Issues* 24:389–96.
McAlpin, Michelle Burge. 1984. "Economic Policy and the True Believer: The Use of Ricardian Rent Theory in the Bombay Survey and Settlement System." *Journal of Economic History* 44:421–27.
Misra, B. R. 1942. *Land Revenue Policy in the United Provinces under British Rule*. Benares: Nand Kishore.
Moon, Penderel. 1945. *Strangers in India*. New York: Reynal and Hitchcock.
Nair, Kusum. 1979. *In Defense of the Irrational Peasant*. Chicago: University of Chicago Press.
Neale, Walter C. 1962. *Economic Change in Rural India: Land Tenure and Reform in Uttar Pradesh, 1880–1955*. New Haven: Yale University Press. Reprint Port Washington, NY, and London: Kennikat Press, 1973.
———. 1972. "The Marginal Laborer and the Harijan in Rural India." In *The Untouchables in Contemporary India*, edited by J. Michael Mahar, 57–66. Tucson: University of Arizona Press.
———. 1988. "Land Tenure, Revenue, and Reform in South Asia." In *Encyclopedia of Asian History*. Vol. 2, edited by Ainslee T. Embree, 394–397. New York: Charles Scribner's Sons.
Neale, Walter C., and Rex M. Edwards. 1983. "Progress and Insecurity, Class and Conflict in Rural India." *Journal of Economic Issues* 17:397–404.
Polanyi, Karl. 1944. *The Great Transformation*. New York: Holt Rinehart and Winston.
Rudolph, Suzanne Hoeber, and Lloyd Rudolph. 1980. "The Centrist Future of Indian Politics." *Asian Survey* 20:575–594.
Stokes, Eric. 1959. *The English Utilitarians and India*. London: Oxford University Press.
Thorner, Daniel. 1976 [1956]. *The Agrarian Prospect in India*. 2d ed. Bombay: Allied Publishers.
———. 1980. *The Shaping of Modern India*. New Delhi: Allied Publishers Private Limited.
U.P. Code. 1939. *A Collection of the Acts Passed by the Governor General of India in Council*. Allahabad: Superintendent, Government Press, U.P.
———. 1951. U.P. *Zamindari Abolition and Land Reforms Act, 1950*. Allahabad: Superintendent, Government Printing and Stationery, U.P.
Wiser, William H. 1936. *The Hindu Jajmani System*. Lucknow: Lucknow Publishing House.
Wiser, William H., and Charlotte M. Wiser. 1963 [1930]. *Behind Mud Walls*. Rev. ed. Berkeley: University of California Press.
Wrigley, E. A. 1988. "Two Kinds of Capitalism, Two Kinds of Growth." *L.S.E. Quarterly* 2:97–121.

# Time and the Economy in a Northeastern Kentucky Region*

## Rhoda Halperin

Time is a dimension of economic organization in all cultures. All processes of material provisioning — production, distribution, and consumption — involve time and timing. Time is also implicit in some of the traditional topics in economic anthropology: periodic marketplace systems, seasonal production regimes, and cycles of crop rotation, to name only a few. Yet time in all of its dimensions either has been treated very narrowly or has been largely assumed or ignored by economic anthropologists, who, coming from cultural anthropology, have tended to work until recently in relatively small time frames. It is still rare, for example, to find a group or a village studied ethnographically at more than one point in time. How did these views of time affect the study of economies? What kinds of temporal categories, if any, came out of these perspectives?

This paper will use one case from northeastern Kentucky to provide some substantive perspectives on the time frames within which economic processes are organized and within which they change. It will examine some of the time concepts embedded in Polanyi's work and some of the ways in which the concept of time could be used to refine and elaborate the theory of the forms of economic integration. While this paper will focus on householding, we can appreciate that processes of reciprocity, redistribution, and exchange, as well as

---

* *An early version of this paper was read at the fourth International Karl Polanyi Conference, held in Montréal in November 1992.*

householding, will vary depending upon the time frames within which they are carried out. Historical and evolutionary time, linear and cyclical time,[1] seasonal time,[2] and life course[3] are some of the kinds of time frames to keep in mind. Whether economic processes such as resource allocation and production itself occur over long or short time periods, or whether exchange processes can be delayed or prolonged, all figure in the shape of economic organization. In all economies, productive work must be scheduled and resources allocated and placed in definite order. There are periodicities to production and distribution processes, just as there are rhythms to storage and consumption. Do similarities in time and timing tell us anything about similarities in economic organization? How can we understand and use time frames to model economic processes?

Johannes Fabian's book *Time and the Other*,[4] an essay on the uses of time in anthropological discourses, is the springboard for this paper. In a manner perhaps unintended by Fabian, his book raises questions about the temporal dimensions of the economy that can be addressed using a substantivist perspective. Polanyi's ideas about the historical development of the market economy, and his strong "transformative" emphasis, most explicit in *The Great Transformation*[5] but also found elsewhere in his work, suggest that Polanyi's models of the economy (from his most general and abstract to his most specific) contain concepts about time that have not been explicated. For example, locational and appropriational movements, the basis for his generic model of the economy,[6] all involve duration as well as sequencing. These time concepts must be made explicit if the full benefits of his cross-cultural, comparative approaches to economic organization are to be realized and used by archaeologists, ethnohistorians, and ethnographers. At the same time, we must not confine our discussions of time and the economy to Polanyi, for now we are at a point in economic anthropology where we can elaborate Polanyi's models beyond what was possible in the 1950s.

The anthropological literature has seen a recent flurry of interest in analysis of time in cultural systems.[7] With only a few exceptions,[8] however, this analysis has been connected to symbolic systems, not to material ones, and the question of time and the economy in everyday life has not been addressed. Neither has the analysis of time and the economy been connected systematically to the institutional arrangements that organize economic processes. This is where Polanyi's concepts, especially his concept of householding, can be most useful.

I will look at the timing of a complicated livelihood strategy designed to both use and resist capitalism in a region of northeastern Kentucky. Here, non-capitalist forms of economic organization dominate capitalist ones while at the same time non-capitalist forms use and manipulate capitalist forms. Resistance to dependency on capitalism involves a fine-tuned, sophisticated system of timing of productive and distributive activities in a series of economic sectors — farms and gardens, a rotating periodic marketplace system (flea markets), and a system of factory-based wage labour, most of it temporary. Elsewhere[9] I have referred to this complicated form of resistance as householding — a concept of Polanyi's but one that he did not elaborate sufficiently or clearly.

Householding involves precise and intricate timing because it co-ordinates so many disparate forms of economic organization. As a form of economic organization, householding has the capacity to deal with complex economic processes, especially the articulation of institutional arrangements. As a concept, householding is especially suited to the analysis of non-capitalist forms of economic organization that persist, grow, and change in the midst of capitalist and post-capitalist economies. Householding has two key features: firstly, it is a strategy of self-sufficiency, and secondly, it is the primary provisioning strategy used by rurally based, three-generational, extended families to resist domination by (and/or capitulation to) industrial capitalism.

## Schedules in the Shallow Rural

Factories, flea markets, and farms and gardens all have their own schedules. Seasonal cycles, family life cycles, and cycles of employment and unemployment, as well as the vagaries of State supports and subsidies for the prices of cash crops such as tobacco, all affect the timing of people's work. In order to participate in and effectively use all three sectors, people must deal with a variety of institutional arrangements in State systems: market and non-market, rural and urban, domestic and public, agrarian and industrial, formal and informal, etc. Regionally based kin networks are the units of analysis in this regional context.

From the point of view of the timing of economic processes, the part of the region that I call the Shallow Rural is the most analytically problematic, as well as the most interesting. It is an unstudied, unnamed, and uncategorized grey area between country and city that contains an intricate mix of livelihood strategies. A rotating periodic marketplace system and factories requiring temporary wage labour are located in the Shallow Rural; so, too, are small farms and rural homesteads with gardens. The Shallow Rural is predominantly rural in the sense that people own small amounts of land and still maintain kitchen gardens. Some people keep small amounts of livestock as well. The average homestead in Shallow Rural hamlets occupies one acre of land that in most cases includes a subsistence garden plot tended by family members. The composition of the homesteads varies and is a factor in who works, when, and at what sorts of tasks. In some cases, the entire extended family can be found in a cluster of households on a homestead. In most cases, however, people in hamlets interact economically in complex ways with kin dispersed throughout the region. Travel time must be calculated carefully.

This Shallow Rural middle ground exhibits a complex infrastructure of highways, as well as shopping malls, an industrial park, housing developments, and mobile-home parks. People who live in the Shallow Rural are migrants from the Deep Rural parts of the region ("the country," in folk parlance). The Deep Rural is a solidly agrarian area. In contrast to the Deep Rural, where options for livelihood are limited to the agrarian sector, the Shallow Rural provides access to many options. Its proximity to the city also affords opportunities for earning cash that are not easily available in the Deep Rural.

In the Shallow Rural, the pattern of householding comprises three arenas or settings, each of which constitutes a way of organizing productive processes, with its own labour requirements and organizational principles. The three are: 1) residential settings such as hamlets, which are the sites of small farms and rural homesteads with subsistence gardens; 2) the periodic marketplace system, which generates cash and provides inexpensive necessities ranging from food and clothing to farm tools and garden equipment; and 3) the wage-labour sector, primarily light-industry factories, most of which are located in an industrial park in the Shallow Rural, but also fast-food outlets and small shops. Taken together, these three economic arenas support the three-generational family networks.

The arenas themselves are complex, and the fact that people use all three and frequently move among them points to the intricacy of the householding system. While the gardens clearly represent a non-capitalist form of economic organization using exclusively family labour, the marketplaces represent a mix of capitalist and non-capitalist elements. Family labour is used in the vendors' booths, but the goods enter the marketplaces via a variety of capitalist as well as non-capitalist paths. Some of the new goods are simply the cast-offs of the capitalist system — for example, Levi jeans with uneven stitching or bottles of salad dressing with expired dates. (This latter example raises interesting considerations with respect to timing.) People gather goods that are obsolete by keeping their eyes open for businesses, such as small grocery stores, that are closing or going bankrupt. One finds pencils bearing the name of a defunct company, for example, quite often in flea markets. Other goods sold in marketplaces are the products of non-capitalist productive relations of many sorts, from used clothing to crafts made by unpaid family labour.

The rotating periodic marketplace system is extensive and elaborate.[10] The major markets are large; one is now located in a former tobacco warehouse. There are three major markets in the region, located as far apart as fifty miles along an interstate highway. Major markets meet on Saturdays and Sundays; other markets only once a week. Intermediate and minor markets tend to cluster near major markets and often feature auctions. These smaller markets are located on county and local roads.[11]

Householding in the Shallow Rural is regionally based. Members of the same extended family will sell goods in the periodic marketplace system; they must therefore secure the goods, and they may also have to process or repair the goods before they can be sold. By the time they reach adulthood, most people also have had some experience in the wage-labour sector. Other means of generating cash in Shallow Rural hamlets are small, family-owned and -run businesses. Many of the men also perform odd jobs within and outside the Shallow Rural. Related males commonly work in pairs; this requires that there be no time conflicts — a young man, for example, may help his father or an uncle with a remodelling project without having the work conflict with a wage-labour job in a factory. In addition, people in hamlets exchange vegetables, home-canned produce, and used household items as well as labour for a variety of purposes such as child care. Hamlet residents share goods when they have an excess or in order to trade goods and services.

The following case will illustrate the regionally-based pattern of householding in the Shallow Rural area. The family network is spread over the region — members may all reside in the same hamlet; some may reside in another Shallow Rural county; yet others may still live in the Deep Rural. The unit of householding, the members of which must co-ordinate their economic activities, is the bilateral, three- or four-generation kin network. As we will see, householding co-ordinates multiple livelihood strategies in multiple institutional arrangements: farms, gardens, marketplaces, and wage-labour establishments (factories, restaurants). Because people may be spread over long distances, timing and co-ordinating of tasks are critical.

**The Smith Family**

Harry and Ilene Smith, both in their late sixties, live on the main road running through a hamlet in the Shallow Rural. They have one daughter, Sue, who is married to Nathan, a carpenter. Sue and Nathan have two children and live in a mobile-home park about six miles from the hamlet. On a typical fall weekend, these economic activities must be co-ordinated: Harry usually has two or three odd jobs, such as house-painting and/or renovating. The jobs must be completed before the weather turns too cold for outside work. Harry and Ilene are regular vendors in the periodic marketplace system, and in the fall they are eager to sell off the goods they have accumulated over the summer from auctions and garage sales; the best days to sell at the major marketplaces are Saturdays and Sundays. In the fall, Ilene is also concerned with "putting up" her beans and cucumbers for the winter. If she does not process them in time, the vegetables will grow tough and too large.

On one particular fall weekend, Ilene's sister, Kate, who lives on a farm in the Deep Rural part of the region (the country), has taken ill, and Ilene must take her some cooked food during the weekend. Ilene and Harry decide to sell their goods at one of the major marketplaces on Saturday, the busiest day. They take their grandchildren with them because Sue and Nathan, who work as temporary wage labourers in a nearby factory, will harvest Ilene's beans and cucumbers and prepare food to take to Ilene's sister after their shift on Saturday. They work six days a week on varying shifts. Sometimes they work double shifts. Nevertheless, Sue feels responsible for her parents' well-being and for the well-being of the relatives of her parents' generation. She says many times that she always makes sure that "Mom and Dad" have a pot of soup or stew on the stove "ready to go." (This means that the food is ready to consume on the spot or can be taken to a needy relative.) On Sunday they will all go to Sue's aunt's farm "in the country" (Deep Rural) for dinner.

**Harry's Family**

Harry was born in 1920. He grew up in a nearby Deep Rural county on a family farm consisting of 300 acres of land and 300 to 400 head of sheep. This was a self-sustaining subsistence farm with a large garden. The Smith family sold the wool from the sheep, a practice that reflects their Scottish roots dating back to the nineteenth century. His sister, ten years younger than Harry, works with her husband, who owns a garage in the region. She spends most of her time driving a truck to bring spare auto parts to the garage. On her excursions around the region, she stops to visit kin, to exchange news and to contribute what she can to her family network. She often brings medicine in exchange for cooked food. Harry's sister has purchased a new house by the river, on good bottom land that benefits from the fertilizer and soil washed down from higher ground. She keeps a large garden.

In his early adult years, Harry walked from his home in the Shallow Rural, across the Ohio River to the Coca Cola plant, where he drove a truck. He held this job for seventeen years. Harry has worked at many different tasks throughout his life, some concurrently. Upon termination of his employment at Coca Cola, his wage-labour jobs included working a water station in his home county. He also stripped furniture, painted houses, repaired typewriters, and raised "bird dogs" for sale — beagles used to hunt rabbits, squirrels, and quail, a major source of protein for people in the Shallow Rural. Harry has passed on his skills to his nephew, Mike, whose father, the owner of the garage and husband of Harry's sister, has little interest in the outdoors. Because Harry visited his sister's homestead often, Mike developed a very close relationship with him. Mike now provides Harry, Ilene, Sue, and Nathan with venison (thirty pounds in summer 1987) in the form of hamburger, steaks, and roasts.

**Ilene's Family Network**

Ilene was born in 1919, one of seven children. Ilene's parents were tenant tobacco farmers. Her paternal uncle lived with the family and everyone worked in the tobacco fields. When she was nine, Ilene began raising turkeys for cash. She also trapped rabbits with her male siblings and sold them to a middleman.

Ilene's family network is extensive. Her sister, Linda Marks, is employed at a craft supplies store in the city. She also operates a home crafts business and, in addition, produces paintings, ceramics, wreaths, refrigerator magnets, etc. Linda can purchase craft items that have been reduced for sale at her place of employment. She also uses her employee discount privilege to purchase goods such as cloth flowers and baskets. Ilene uses these items in the flower arrangements she fashions to sell in the marketplaces (flea markets). The arrangements consist mainly of dried wild flowers and ferns, which she collects and processes regularly. Ilene has a knack for combining a few "store bought" things with items she has acquired at auctions and garage sales or from relatives, who contribute pressed flowers, baskets, and vases for her arrangements.

Linda's daughter, Sally, is employed at the Goody Company (a pseudonym) in Cincinnati. She regularly takes crafts that her mother produces to sell at work. The employees of the Goody Company, especially those in management, often commission Linda to make special items such as flower arrangements. Linda than calls on Ilene to produce extra arrangements. When Linda was starting her business, Lou Ann Rist, Ilene's sister-in-law, also opened a retail business in a well-to-do town in the Shallow Rural. Lou Ann commissions Linda to make crafts for her shop. Ilene also makes pillows, bittersweet wreaths, and flower arrangements to sell at Lou Ann's shop. Linda herself exchanges her crafts with Ilene for fresh garden produce.

### Multiple Livelihood Strategies and Their Timing: Harry and Ilene

Throughout their adulthood, Harry and Ilene have kept a large garden and, until recently, an orchard of pear, plum, peach, cherry, and apple trees. They also grew grapes. The fruit was used for their own consumption and in summer they sold about half of it; much of the fruit was "put up" for the winter in Mason jars. Sue and Nathan collect wild raspberries and blackberries in the summer to supplement the supply of fruit for sale, home consumption, and canning. Sunday dinners in the wintertime are not complete without biscuits and fruit spreads, a form of storage that allows for a supply of fruit over the entire year. All "put up" fruits and vegetables are a form of storage.

In 1970, Harry and Ilene moved to their current, smaller homestead. They gave up the orchard but still keep their large garden. Recently, they began growing large quantities of tomatoes. They sell enough tomatoes to a local restaurant to buy sugar to put up the wild berries for jam. Harry has continued to paint both the interiors and the exteriors of houses in the county in which they now live. Nathan is becoming increasingly involved in Harry's repair work.

Harry and Ilene are regular vendors in the marketplace system. They began selling in 1979. Mostly they participate in the major marketplaces on the weekends. Throughout the week they collect goods and mend, repair, or clean them for sale. They devote Fridays to acquiring items from yard sales and from relatives who may want to get rid of "old things." Ilene has an eye for bargains, and she can transform an old and dirty picture frame or set of dishes into valuable "antiques."

Harry's success is linked to Nathan's ability to keep the wage-labour system at arm's length. After several years as wage labourers, Nathan and Harry have become partners. They perform odd jobs obtained through Harry's extensive regional network. Now that Harry is "getting up in years," Nathan can keep him going by performing the heavy work. Nathan expresses great dislike for all facets of the factory system, and he uses it selectively — only when he is in need of a steady source of cash. Such father/son and son-in-law collaborations are typical of the region. Intergenerational ties are critical to the pattern of householding. Nathan's working for Harry is central to the son-in-law's decision to shift his labour from the wage-labour economy to an arrangement that is more informal and both physically and financially safer. Nathan's decision also accommodates Harry's position in the life course; it parallels rural patterns in that it allows Harry to remain in charge (as would be the case on farms in the Deep Rural, and in Europe prior to migration), yet reduces his workload.

### Resistance to Dependence on Capitalism

People in the Shallow Rural, particularly men, who quit their wage-labour jobs in favour of odd jobs, or who decide to intensify their activities in the agrarian and marketplace sectors, often see themselves as opting out of the system. To the extent that they are releasing themselves from the rigid schedules and often difficult and dangerous routine of factory work, they are freeing themselves. Yet they are committing themselves to other kinds of regimens and constraints. Acquiring goods — from family, garage sales, smaller markets, etc. — and preparing them for sale can be very time-consuming, and this labour must be co-ordinated with other work in the agrarian sector. In addition, time and labour obligations to the kin network can be substantial. Clearly, however, people see their investments in kin networks as providing themselves with economic security (a form of "social storage" of resources) and with the opportunity to leave wage-labour jobs and establish other work combinations.

In one sense, these multiple livelihood strategies were established long ago in response to lay-offs and plant closings; in another sense, people have created new ways of generating cash and providing for their families. Older people in the region decry young adults' lack of agricultural skills. Attitudes about employment and preparation for unemployment vary according to the extent of one's family network and position in the life course. Older workers, for example, many of whom have permanent jobs, feel strongly that the wage labour available to them will soon disappear. Many perceive their jobs as fragile, coming to an end. When the time for wage labour is seen to be short, alternative livelihood strategies must kick in. Older workers become involved in subsistence gardening; they speak with great pride about their gardens. Their alternative cash-generating strategies include selling in marketplaces and performing odd jobs. They encourage their younger kin to work the booths in the marketplaces, especially on Sundays when wage workers are free. Workers with ties to marketplaces and to agrarian economic strategies are much better equipped to use temporary labour selectively. Most temporary workers regard wage work as a means of filling time between odd jobs and of helping out in bad times.

**The Timing of Householding as a Form of Peasant Resistance**

Peasant resistance has become an increasingly important topic in social science.[12] The strategies used by rural people to exercise control over their lives and their means of livelihood can be seen as the orchestration of complicated timing and dovetailing of activities in institutional arrangements that are all on their own schedules. Practical skills (food production, processing, storage), knowledge and use of local resources, and maintenance of intergenerational ties through the meeting of family obligations provide people in the region with a measure of control over their livelihood. Time inputs that are greater than that required to participate in a capitalist economy are often necessary in order to maintain control and flexibility; work schedules are flexible, but people often put in many more than forty hours per week.

Families organize productive tasks within the context of a mainstream capitalist economy without becoming dependent on the capitalist economy for their livelihood. People obtain odd jobs through kin connections; these jobs often involve kin as work partners. In addition to the exchange of labour and goods among kin, there are some extremely subtle ways in which kin relations shape people's economic lives. For example, people who work in factories often do so only until someone in their network provides another option. People quit their jobs often, and they speak with pride of their decision to terminate employment in the mainstream capitalist economy. What may appear to outsiders as irresponsibility, inability to adhere to a rigid time schedule, may simply be the replacement of a wage-labour job with a set of tasks that are safer, that offer better pay and more time flexibility, and that provide independence and a sense of self worth. Sporadic employment is sporadic only from the point of view of one economic sector, the capitalist economy. Young adults become a source of concern to their kin (especially their older male relatives) when they choose to remain in the temporary wage-labour sector to the exclusion of economic activities in the agrarian and/or marketplace sectors. "Putting all your eggs in one basket" is not considered wise. Cash is necessary, not for accumulation or for display, but for purchasing those necessities that cannot be produced or obtained in any other way.

Selecting jobs and work tasks whose timing is harmonious with maintaining kin ties is another form of resistance to capitalism, because it keeps the family provisioning processes going. Family provisioning is the essence of householding. The goal of the familial economy is not to ascend the ladder of social stratification, but rather to keep the kin network intact through everyday, on-going, overlapping, and intertwining economic activities. The kin network offers security against having to depend on any single economic sector. Occupation is secondary in defining who people are: the family network defines self and person. A family imperative guides people's economic activities. Kinship orders livelihood processes through the pattern of householding. These livelihood processes are connected to geographical places, but are not bounded by households or communities.

**Summary and Conclusion**

Householding must be understood as a form of resistance to capitalism and to dependence upon the State.[13] The multiple livelihood structures organized by family networks in this Appalachian region are highly complex ones. The invisibility of this kind of structure is due partly to a family's dispersion throughout the region and partly to subtle and complicated timing devices and co-ordination. The informal nature of the provisioning strategies masks their structure and timing. Flea markets are easy to observe, but they are not easy to understand as part of a rotating periodic marketplace system. It is also not immediately apparent that the marketplace system is only one element in a complex provisioning process. In this respect, marketplaces are public, open arenas with private, hidden agendas and schedules. Members of family networks use the system very carefully; they calculate many variables (seasonality, location) into their buying patterns, their selling locations, and the timing of both. The behaviour of individuals — for example, in quitting a temporary wage-labour job — would also not seem at first to belong to a structured system of provisioning. A parent's brief conversation with a wage-labouring son who passes through a marketplace in a fleeting moment can serve to co-ordinate a large family gathering during which food, goods, services, and information are circulated. Even if no gathering is planned, people can communicate with one another at designated times and places to plan a whole series of activities. These activities encompass both locational and appropriational movements, and they co-ordinate the transportation of goods and the distribution of food, time, and labour. These co-ordination processes give people a degree of control over their livelihood, enabling them to resist dependence upon the capitalist economy. There is wisdom here — a rationality of steadfastness and doggedness that is tremendously resilient, precisely because it is multifaceted.[14]

**Notes**

1. Heidegger 1982.
2. Mauss and Beuchat 1968 [1904–05].
3. Lambek 1990.
4. Fabian 1983.
5. Polanyi 1944.
6. Halperin 1988.
7. Aveni 1989; Munn 1991.
8. Bourdieu 1964; 1977; 1979; 1990; Giddens 1979; 1981; 1984; Weiner 1980; 1985. Even Bourdieu and Giddens treat time and the economy in the abstract.
9. Halperin 1991.
10. Halperin 1990.
11. See Halperin 1990.
12. Scott 1985.
13. Camaroff 1985.
14. Weinberg 1975.

## References

Aveni, Anthony F. 1989. *Empires of Time: Calendars, Clocks and Cultures.* New York: Basic Books.
Bergman, W. 1992. "The Problem of Time in Sociology: An Overview of the Literature on the State of Theory and Research on the 'Sociology of Time,' 1900–82." *Time and Society* 1:81–134.
Bourdieu, Pierre. 1964. "The Attitude of the Algerian Peasant towards Time." In *Mediterranean Countrymen,* edited by J. Pitt-Rivers, 55–72. The Hague: Mouton.
———. 1977. *Outline of a Theory of Practice.* Cambridge: Cambridge University Press.
———. 1979 [1963]. "The Disenchantment of the World." In *Algeria 1960,* 1–94. Cambridge: Cambridge University Press.
———. 1990 [1980]. *The Logic of Practice.* Stanford: Stanford University Press.
Fabian, Johannes. 1983. *Time and the Other: How Anthropology Makes its Object.* New York: Columbia University Press.
Giddens, Anthony. 1979. *Central Problems in Social Theory: Action, Structure and Contradiction in Social Analysis.* Berkeley: University of California Press.
———. 1981. "Time, Labour and the City." In *A Contemporary Critique of Historical Materialism.* Vol. 1, *Power, Property and the State,* 129–65. Berkeley: University of California Press.
———. 1984. *The Constitution of Society: Outline of the Theory of Structuration.* Berkeley: University of California Press.
Halperin, Rhoda. 1988. *Economies across Cultures.* London: Macmillan.
———. 1990. *The Livelihood of Kin: Making Ends Meet "the Kentucky Way."* Austin: University of Texas Press.
———. 1991. "Polanyi's Concept of Householding: Resistance and Livelihood in an Appalachian Region." In *Research in Economic Anthropology* 13, edited by Barry L. Isaac, 93–116. Greenwich, CT: JAI Press.
Heidegger, Martin. 1982. *The Basic Problems of Phenomenology.* Bloomington: Indiana University Press.
Lambek, Michael. 1990. "Exchange, Time and Person in Mayotte." *American Anthropologist* 92:647–71.
Mauss, Marcel, and Henri Beuchat. 1968 [1904–1905]. "Essai sur les variations saisonnières des sociétés Eskimos." In *Sociologie et anthropologie,* Pt. 7, 389–475. Paris: Presses Universitaires de France.
Munn, Nancy D. 1990. "Constructing Regional Worlds in Experience: Kula Exchange, Witchcraft and Gawan Local Events." *Man* 25:1–17.
Polanyi, Karl. 1944. *The Great Transformation.* New York: Holt Rinehart and Winston.
———. 1957. "The Economy as Instituted Process." In *Trade and Market in the Early Empires,* edited by Karl Polanyi, Conrad M. Arensberg, and Harry W. Pearson. Glencoe, IL: Free Press.
Scott, James C. 1985. *Weapons of the Weak: Everyday Forms of Peasant Resistance.* New Haven: Yale University Press.

Weinberg, Daniela. 1975. *Peasant Wisdom: Cultural Adaptation in a Swiss Village.* Berkeley and Los Angeles: University of California Press.

Weiner, Annette B. 1980. "Reproduction: A Replacement for Reciprocity." *American Ethnologist* 7:71–85.

*Also published by*

## TOWARD A HUMANIST POLITICAL ECONOMY
### Harold Chorney and Phillip Hansen

Guided by a critical theory perspective, Chorney and Hansen focus their attention on the neglected cultural side of society in order to chart the progress of political change. They feel that the simple economic explanations and the old radical conventions can no longer be relied on in explaining and pointing the way towards a fundamentally reformed society. Instead, they use as background some of the insights of writers as diverse as Hannah Arendt and John Maynard Keynes.

224 pages, index
Paperback ISBN:1-895431-22-0    $19.95
Hardcover ISBN:1-895431-23-9    $38.95

## POLITICAL ECOLOGY
*Beyond Environmentalism*
### Dimitrios I. Roussopoulos

Examining the perspective offered by various components of political ecology, this book presents an overview of its origins as well as its social and cultural causes. It summarizes the differences, and similarities, between political ecology and social ecology, while revealing, quite candidly, that the resolution of the present planetary crisis hinges on the outcome and consequences of this new politics.

180 pages
Paperback ISBN: 1-895431-80-8    $15.95
Hardcover ISBN: 1-895431-81-6    $34.95

## HOT MONEY AND THE POLITICS OF DEBT *2nd edition*
### R.T. Naylor

...*a wide angle view of the seamy side of international finance.*
**New York Times**

*As conspiracy theories go, here is one that is truly elegant. It involves everybody...all playing a dirty global game of take the money and run.*
**Washington Post**

...*a fascinating survey of international finance scams that are aided and abedded by players as diverse as the Vatican, international banks and the denizens of various tax havens around the world.*
**Globe and Mail**

510 pages, index
Paperback ISBN: 1-895431-94-8    $19.99
Hardcover ISBN: 1-895431-95-6    $38.99

**CRITICAL PERSPECTIVES ON HISTORIC ISSUES**
This series, from the work of the *Karl Polanyi Institute of Political Economy* at Concordia University in Montréal, is intended to present important research by leading international scholars and critics.

**The Life and Work of Karl Polanyi,** *edited by Kari Polanyi-Levitt*
**Culture and Social Change,** *edited by Colin Leys and Marguerite Mendell*
**Humanity, Society and Commitment,** *edited by Kenneth McRobbie,*
**Europe: Central and East,** *edited by Marguerite Mendell and Klaus Nielsen*
**Artful Practices: The Political Economy of Everyday Life,** *edited by Henri Lustiger-Thaler and Daniel Salée*
**The Milano Papers,** *edited by Michele Cangiani*

## BLACK ROSE BOOKS
*has also published the following books of related interest*

The Political Economy of International Labour Migration, *by Hassan N. Gardezi*
Private Interest, Public Spending, *by William E. Scheurerman and Sidney Plotkin*
Dissidence: Essays Against the Mainstream, *by Dimitrios Rousspoulos*
Shock Waves: Eastern Europe After the Revolutions, *by John Feffer*
Ethics, *by Peter Kropotkin*
Mutual Aid, *by Peter Kropotkin*
Political Arrangements: Power and the City, *edited by Henri Lustiger-Thaler*
Bringing the Economy Home From the Market, *by Ross Dobson*
The Myth of the Market: Promises and Illusions, *by Jeremy Seabrook*
Race, Gender and Work: A Multi-Cultural Economic History of Women in the United States, *by Teresa Amott and Julie Matthaei*
Dominion of Debt: Centre, Periphery and the International Economic Order, *by Jeremy Brecher and Tim Costello*
Bankers, Bagmen and Bandits: Business and Politics in the Age of Greed, *by R.T. Naylor*
The Economy of Canada: A Study of Ownership and Control, *by Jorge Niosi*
Essays on Marx's Theory of Value, *by Issak Illich Rubin*

send for a free catalogue of all our titles
BLACK ROSE BOOKS
P.O. Box 1258
Succ. Place du Parc
Montréal, Québec
H3W 2R3 Canada

Printed by the workers of
Les Ateliers Graphiques Marc Veilleux Inc.
Cap Saint-Ignace, Québec
for Black Rose Books Ltd.